THE
GALLOPING MAJOR

THE
GALLOPING MAJOR

MY LIFE AND SINGULAR TIMES

RONALD FERGUSON

M

MACMILLAN
LONDON

First published 1994 by Macmillan London

an imprint of Macmillan General Books
Cavaye Place London SW10 9PG
and Basingstoke

Associated companies throughout the world

ISBN 0-333-61454-2

1 3 5 7 9 8 6 4 2

A CIP catalogue record for this book is available
from the British Library

Photoset by Parker Typesetting Service, Leicester
Printed by Mackays of Chatham PLC,
Chatham, Kent

Dedication

To the women in my life. My mother, Susan, Jane, Sarah, Alice, Eliza and my son Andrew with all my love and grateful appreciation of your devotion.

Contents

Acknowledgements

There are many people whom I should like to thank for helping to make this book possible. First and foremost, it could not have happened without Caroline Richards, whose way with words often transcended mine, and who made bullying by fax into an art form. It was Jilly Cooper who first encouraged me in the project; gratifyingly, both she and Desmond Elliott, my agent, thought it was a good idea, and I'm grateful to Desmond for his wit and enthusiasm, and for putting me in touch with Caroline. Desmond's assistant, Lisa Moylett, provided much excellent help, and I'd like to thank Jane Wood, my editor, for being so patient. My wife Sue helped me combat chronic amnesia concerning our early years together, and my mother, Lady Marian Elmhirst, has been a tower of strength about intricate family history and childhood details. Thanks too go to Michael Borlase, my farm manager, and those of my friends who have stood firmly by me through my various trials and tribulations. My late, great friend Willie Loyd was a staunch provider of details of our mutual military past stretching back over forty years, more of which is chronicled in his excellent book, *Challengers and Chargers*. My older daughters Jane and Sarah, possibly against their better judgement, encouraged me to go ahead, and I'd like to thank them, my wife Sue, and my three younger children, Andrew, Alice and Eliza, for all the joy and happiness they bring to my life every day.

Picture Acknowledgements

The publishers would like to acknowledge the following copyright holders, with grateful thanks:

Camera Press: Section 3 – Page 5, top right
Desmond O'Neill: Section 1 – Page 6, bottom left
Richard Greenly: Section 4 – Page 4, top; Page 4, bottom left
Glenn Harvey Print Association: Section 4 – Page 8, top
Hello! Magazine: Section 4 – Page 7, bottom
Lord Lichfield: Section 3 – Page 3, bottom left; Page 3, bottom right
Terry O'Neill: Section 4 – Page 3, bottom
The Press Association: Section 4 – Page 5, top left and top right
Mike Roberts: Section 3 – Page 5, bottom; Page 7, top; Page 7, middle; Page 8, top; Section 4 – Page 3, middle; Page 5, bottom; Page 6, bottom

Author's Pre-Foreword

MAJOR WILLIAM LOYD, 1937–1994

The Life Guards

It was with very great sadness that my true and loyal friend Willie Loyd was too ill to write a foreword to my book.

He had very kindly agreed not only to write a foreword but also to edit the military and polo facts.

Willie, I sincerely thank you for your friendship and loyalty over forty years.

Foreword

One of the first columns I produced for the *Sunday Times* back in 1969 was on the tribulations of being a cricket wife. Towards the end of the piece, however, I relented and admitted some matches were more amusing than others.

'The Household Brigade is always good for a giggle,' I wrote. 'Last year, there was a languid Major who whenever he failed to stop the ball turned to a man fielding next to him and rapped out: "Fetch it, Corporal."'

The languid Major was Ronald Ferguson – even in those days he had panache.

I next wrote about the Major in 1986, while covering Sarah Ferguson's wedding to Prince Andrew for the *Mail on Sunday*. There cannot have been a prouder father in the world as, with russet eyebrows flying more merrily than any buttress, he led the nation's darling up the aisle.

It was a glorious wedding. We all warmed our hands on it. Fergie Fever had reached an all time high. The love between the handsome young couple was palpable. They made their vows with true conviction and after each 'I will', we could hear a great muffled roar of approval from the crowds outside the Abbey.

Two years later, I embarked on a novel about polo. Ronald was by now a household name, both as the father of the Duchess of York and as Prince Charles's extremely efficient polo manager. It was with great trepidation, therefore, that I wrote to him, asking him if I could pick his brains, and suggesting lunch. Return of post, he accepted.

We went to the Hyde Park Hotel. From Ronald's public image, I expected him to be somewhat brusque, high-handed and blimpish with a very short fuse. Desperately nervous, I booked a table by the window, so he could at least admire a fine view of the park if he got bored. I was further unnerved when he announced on arrival that he didn't drink. How on earth could we break the ice?

In fact we didn't draw breath for nearly two and a half hours. In the flesh, Ronald was far more handsome than his photographs. He was also utterly charming, modest, totally unpompous, possessing a splendid sense of the ridiculous which he frequently turned on himself, blissfully full of gossip but never malicious, and tremendous fun.

I floated home, my head swimming with wonderful polo anecdotes, my notebook crammed with crucial contacts which opened doors for me all over England as well as in Palm Beach and Argentina. More importantly, I felt I had made a marvellous new friend.

Through the next three years while I was writing the book, Ronald always made time at matches and on the telephone to answer my questions and point me in the right direction. I think all his friends would agree that he is also a true friend if one is unhappy or in any kind of trouble.

I was therefore delighted to be able to repay some of his kindness by writing the foreword to *The Galloping Major*, the story of his life, which I truly enjoyed reading.

But I also accepted this commission with great sadness, aware that Ronald's first choice to introduce his book had been his great friend Major Willie Loyd.

The former polo correspondent of the *Daily Telegraph*, Willie had recently published his first non-fiction book *Challengers and Chargers*, a history of The Life Guards.

He had also written his first novel, *A Lurcher in the House* and had just embarked on Ronald's foreword, when he died at the tragically early age of fifty-six . . . Whom the Gods love.

Willie was not only a darling man, but also a colossal tease. His long friendship with Ronald was based on endless affectionate banter. Together – a wonderful double act known as 'Pinky and Perky' – they ran the Guards Polo Club at Smith's Lawn, raising it over the years literally to a pitch of perfection, culminating in the Cartier International days of the late eighties. On these occasions Ronald used to stride round the field, blazer buttons twinkling like the Pleiades, barking out instructions on his walkie-talkie, eagle eye never missing a blade of grass or a dashing young blade that was out of place.

According to Willie's wife, Lilo: 'Willie (Pinky) and Ronald (Perky) first crossed paths when they played polo for the Life Guards and won both the Captain's and Subaltern's Cup and the Inter-Regimental Trophy in 1963.' The glamorous pair were then sent to Cyprus in 1964, 'to keep the peace between the Greeks and Turks and pleasure the RAF wives from all accounts'. Ronald was a bit late to take over his command of 'A' Squadron, since he was playing polo in Pakistan.

As Willie put it, 'Every Squadron Leader with an independent command will run it as a private army. Ronald, possessing both a determined streak and a superiority complex, ran a relaxed but efficient team. He also had all the style with a self-designed red pennant on his vehicle and a personal trumpeter.'

It was in Cyprus too, according to Willie, that Ronald used 'to clean out the local pharmacies of Elizabeth Arden suncreams, since he incessantly annointed his Adonis-like body in order not to burn'.

Willie also intended to relate the hilarious story of a potential Household Brigade Drum horse, which later became known as Ferguson's Folly. This massive skewbald, which Ronald had selected from Ireland, completed full training with practice drums, before buckling at the knees on the big day when invited to bear the full weight of William IV silver drums.

What a funny and affectionate foreword Willie would have written had he had time to complete it.

What Willie and I did share, after all the splendours and joys of Sarah's wedding, was our sadness and dismay, when suddenly the Ferguson family seemed to be beset by a series of disasters more suited to the House of Atreus.

To cheer his friend on a dark day, Willie even joked that he was having to write so often to commiserate with Ronald on yet another dastardly press mauling, that he was thinking of getting a standard letter run off on the word processor.

In *The Galloping Major*, Ronald tells us how things went so wrong. It was inevitable, probably, that the passionate love affair between the British public and the Duchess of York, largely initiated by the media, would prove too hot not to cool down. Such is the churlish nature of our national press that as soon as they have built up a public idol, they embark on a savage hunt for its clay feet.

This obsessive media attention is one of the more nightmarish aspects of joining the Royal Family. How could any one remain normal if, relentlessly each day, their hair, their clothes, their make-up, their weight, their voice, their mannerisms were criticized, and their slightest utterance misquoted or ridiculed. In addition, they would have to read endless sanctimonious, speculative claptrap about their marriage and relationships with other members of the Royal Family. Even worse, they would be expected to endure this bombardment of arrows as unflinchingly as St Sebastian.

It comes as little surprise that victims crack under the strain, and we witness Prince Charles justifying himself to Jonathan Dimbleby for two and a half hours or Princess Diana encouraging her friends to spill the beans to Andrew Morton. Small wonder Sarah's marriage to Prince Andrew slowly came unstuck, particularly when he was so often away at sea and unable to provide comfort and boost morale.

This press bullying must have been almost worse for a devoted father like Ronald. He is honest about the catastrophes that subsequently hit his family and takes the blame for many of them, but admits, 'that it was not my actions, but the way they were interpreted by the press, that most hurt my family'.

The Galloping Major is therefore on the one hand a very temperate attempt to set the record straight, to show the Ferguson family in honest focus, not through a long lens darkly.

On the other hand, it is also a fascinating account of Ronald's grand and eccentric family, his school and army days, his polo playing adventures, his marriages, how he brought up his two daughters single-handed after his first wife left him, and in turn about their subsequent marriages.

He was also in a unique position to observe the Royal Family at close quarters over a number of years, and gives us riveting details about Prince Philip as a father, of staying at Windsor and having the Queen back to dinner at Lowood in Ascot. On a more frivolous level, we learn what aftershave Ronald wore to take Sarah up the aisle, and how his Jack Russell, 'Mr Bugs', avenged the family honour on a door-stepping reporter.

Most of his vitriol is reserved for the palace equerries who, when the rest of the world were hailing Fergie as a breath of fresh air, remained resolutely allergic to draughts. He paints a chilling picture of Sarah like a butterfly enmeshed in a spider's web of palace red tape. The more she tried to please, the more the old tabby cats disapproved.

The heroine of *The Galloping Major*, however, must be Sue, the second Mrs Ferguson, unassailable proof that beauty can live with kindness. 'An honourable, true and loving wife', she took on a mad March hare and two volatile step-daughters, bore Ronald three more most attractive children and remained utterly staunch and loyal, holding the family together during its darkest days. Ronald knows this. In one of the most touching passages, he has dedicated his book to her and his children.

Ultimately though, this is a cheerful and optimistic tale, about an intensely human man, who has been stitched up so often that, like a favourite teddy, he is more stitch and patch than bear, but who remains lovable and always bounces back.

As he claims he has given up polo in favour of a new career in cricket, I hope the only galloping the Major does in future is straight up the best-seller lists.

Jilly Cooper

Prologue

'WHO THE HELL is standing on my train?' The words rang out loud and clear from the top of the main staircase in Clarence House. I looked up in astonishment. Poised in mid-descent, looking more lovely than I could ever have imagined, stood my second daughter Sarah. Dressed in a sumptuous cream silk wedding gown, her hair and make-up immaculately done, she turned the full fury of her wrath on a hapless leaden-footed attendant. I let out a huge sigh of relief. I had arrived at the Queen Mother's official residence several hours earlier with no idea how Sarah was feeling. Was she going to be terribly nervous? Would I need to buck her up? Calm her down? How would she cope with the hugely taxing ceremonial occasion that was in front of her? As soon as she came down the stairs, with that expression on her face, I knew she was home and dry. There was nothing to worry about. Sarah could face it all, with supreme confidence. Even though she was about to marry a prince, my daughter was not going to play the role of the blushing bride. As I looked up at her, my heart swelled with pride, for her sheer gutsiness, for daring to be different. She'd be a huge asset, I thought, this feisty daughter of mine, to a family who tended towards introspection.

The advance wedding party, including the bridesmaids and pages, had left several minutes before. The crowds, lining the Mall ten or twelve deep, were roaring for us. 'Sarah! Sarah!' The noise was almost deafening as we climbed carefully into the beautiful gilded coach that would carry us along the wedding route to Westminster Abbey. I nodded and smiled to the Life Guards who were escorting us, remembering the days when it had been me who rode alongside a royal coach, in exactly the same role. It was such a strange feeling now to be on the inside looking out. I turned to my daughter as we surveyed the massive crowd. 'Isn't it incredible?' I said. 'All these people have come here just to see my little daughter.'

As we approached the Abbey, I did begin to feel a flutter of nerves. Somehow this great royal occasion, which had been months in the planning, endless in the rehearsing, had now become a reality. As we stood at the entrance to the aisle, at the great West Door of the Abbey, I helped Sarah straighten that troublesome train. There was still no sign of nerves. 'Dads,' she whispered urgently, 'do you know which way to go?'

'Of course,' I replied. 'Just follow the blue carpet.'

Little did I know that morning of Wednesday 23 July 1986, as we took the four-minute walk up that formidably grand aisle, that this fairy-tale royal wedding would bring so much sadness in its wake. Little did I realize that, far from being welcomed as a much needed breath of fresh air, my daughter would eventually be criticized and shunned. I couldn't guess at the number of mistakes she would subsequently make in trying to do things right, or that this marriage between two young people who cared so deeply about each other would end, painfully and publicly, just six short years later. Neither could I foresee then the enormous impact this wedding would have on my own life. By becoming a 'media figure', I'd be an easy target to shoot down. If you believe the tabloids, in time it would be alleged that I heaped shame and humiliation on our family. There would follow a kind of 'ethnic cleansing' of Fergusons by the Royal Family, even though we had been associated with them and served them loyally over several generations. My long-term association with my beloved game of polo in this country would cease, as would my duties as Polo Manager to the Prince of Wales, and I would be ostracized by many of my so-called friends.

What went wrong? When did the fairy-tale turn into the nightmare? I don't mind admitting that I made a lot of mistakes along the way, and there are many things I regret. One of the many ironies of life, it has been said, is that it has to be lived forwards, but can only be understood backwards – certainly true in my case. I've been too gullible, my reflexes too slow to dodge the ammunition.

I have never spoken out before, but rather than stand condemned, I have decided to write this book in the hope that it will go some way towards setting the record straight.

Do not be sorry that roses have thorns,
be thankful that thorns have roses.

CHAPTER ONE

Early Childhood, and a Memory of My Father

I WAS BORN at home in 1931, on my father's birthday, 10 October. I weighed in at ten and a half pounds, which can't have been much fun for my mother. My parents then lived at Cumberland Terrace, Regent's Park, in an elegant Regency house which was ideally situated for my father; as a serving officer in the Life Guards, he was based at Albany Barracks just behind the park. Although I spent my first few months in London, we soon moved to Lodge Farm, Kineton, Warwickshire, roughly midway between Leamington Spa and Banbury, with my brother, John, who had been born two years before me. Lodge Farm was the setting for an idyllic early childhood. I remember it as an enormous grey stone-built house approached from a very long drive, a house where all the rooms were spacious and airy, with high ceilings and huge windows. Like Dummer, my present home, the farm buildings were relatively close to the house, which was surrounded by beautiful gardens, traditional herbaceous borders with roses and delphiniums that gave a blaze of colour all summer long.

In 1942, my father Andrew was given command of the Life Guards, as his father, Brigadier General Algernon Ferguson, had been before him. My paternal grandparents lived at Polebrooke Hall, near Oundle in Northamptonshire, a rather grand baronial hall, although as children we took its size and grandeur for granted. My great-grandfather too had commanded

1

the Life Guards – he was Colonel John Stephenson Ferguson of the 2nd Life Guards, who had married the Honourable Margaret Brand, eldest daughter of the second Viscount Hampden. Through her, we can trace our ancestors right back to Charles II, the first of many connections my family has had with the British royal family.

My father was one of four children – he had a brother Victor, and two sisters, Jane and Susan. My Ferguson grand-parents were kind, supportive, gentle people who spoiled me rotten. I remember many happy visits to Polebrooke Hall; it was dark and spooky, with plenty of cellars and old fashioned stables where one could play hide-and-seek for hours.

During the course of his army career, my father Andrew had acquired the nickname of Fergie though it has never been used within the family to refer to anyone since, certainly not my daughter Sarah.

My mother was born Marian Louisa Montagu Douglas Scott, daughter of Lord Herbert Montagu Douglas Scott, the fifth son of the 6th Duke of Buccleugh. Her family's roots can also be traced back to Charles II; she and my father were already distant cousins before their marriage. Mother was a first cousin of Princess Alice, the Dowager Duchess of Glou-cester, whose maiden name was Montagu Douglas Scott.

My maternal grandfather had a successful career in the City, and had been chairman of Rolls-Royce and associated with many city companies. He was proud to have been appointed Gentleman at Arms, one of the attendants who escort the monarch into Parliament at the opening of each session. This meant that my mother was presented at Court twice: as a débutante, as was customary in those days, and also upon her marriage.

I say all this to illustrate how wrong some of the news-papers have been about our family background, suggesting we used Sarah's marriage to better ourselves socially. It is obviously nonsense. To my amusement, Mother's family have always regarded their Buccleugh lineage as being socially superior to that of the Windsors! There are many instances in family archives of acquaintances with various members of Royal Family: press clippings in one of the photo albums, for instance, give detailed reports of a private visit made by the Prince and Princess of Teck to Polebrooke Hall at the turn of the century for a weekend house party.

Although my parents shared the same first cousins, they had never met as children. They first encountered each other at a regimental dance at Aldershot, and the meeting was engineered by Father's sister Jane, who was one of my mother's best friends. This aunt, Jane Ferguson, was later to marry the Queen's agent at Sandringham, Sir William Fellowes. Their son, Sir Robert Fellowes, who is my first cousin, is currently the Queen's private secretary. He is married to another Jane, the former Lady Jane Spencer, elder sister of the Princess of Wales.

Family legend has it that shortly after she met my father, Mother was off to stay with one of her first cousins for the Grand National. My father – who rarely sought a social life – reportedly begged my mother to take him with her. And that, she assures me, is how their courtship began.

Grandfather Ferguson was very Victorian, very much the Brigadier. The first time my mother met him it was at tea at Polebrooke Hall, when my father was being very tiresome, dithering over which cake to have. Bravely, she said, 'Who cares which cake you have?' 'That', said my grandfather, turning to my grandmother, 'is the person for Andrew to marry.'

When they did marry, in 1927, the present Duke of Buccleugh was a page at their wedding. They honeymooned in Monte Carlo where Mother, still only nineteen and therefore under age, had to be left outside the gambling rooms while her new husband went in for a flutter.

Now, at eighty-six, my mother is still as sprightly and determined as she was then. Although she has been an accomplished and talented horsewoman all her life, from an early age she has also been fascinated with motor cars. When Mother was about seven her parents were puzzled as to why their luncheon guests often refused a repeat invitation. Banished from the table, bored with the nursery alternative, the young Marian had developed a new pastime. She would take the guests' cars and drive them around the estate. On several occasions she drove vehicles into the bushes and had to be rescued by an irate chauffeur. When she was eventually old enough to hold a legal driving licence, her father asked if she would like to become a demonstration driver for his company Rolls-Royce. She jumped at the chance and passed their top chauffeurs' test with flying colours. In those days, test drivers only worked on certain days. Mother's was a Monday, but one day the showroom received a message from one prospective customer who wanted Miss Marian Scott to take him out on a Wednesday.

'Certainly not,' said my grandfather. 'Her day is Monday.'

'Then I regret that my boss won't be interested in buying a car,' the secretary explained.

'All right,' said my grandfather to Mother. 'You'd better do it.'

It was a bright, sunny day and Mother and the gentleman drove out to Burnham Beeches in Buckinghamshire. He got out of the car, spread a rug on the ground and brought out a Fortnum & Mason picnic hamper crammed full of good things to eat and drink. Mother panicked slightly. 'I've got to go now,' she said. 'I've got to take somebody else out, I have another appointment.'

Later, she innocently told her father about the incident. 'I think Mr X was keener on me than he was on the car.' Grandfather was furious and immediately put a stop to all her test driving duties, although by then she had sold fifteen

Rolls-Royces. She was also quite an expert on car mechanics, and often infuriated Grandfather by being able to start a car when he couldn't.

Her mother Marie was Irish, from County Cork, and a terrific character. They owned a little cottage in Horsham in Sussex and on one occasion, when she had been to London for the day, Granny Scott arrived back at Horsham station in the evening to discover dense fog and no sign of a taxi.

My grandfather was away on business, so my grandmother rang Mother, who was then aged about fifteen.

'I can't spend the night in the waiting room,' she said to her daughter. 'No taxi will bring me out.'

'Stay there,' was Mother's response. 'I'll come and fetch you.'

And she did just that, driving the Rolls-Royce through narrow country lanes in the thickest blanket of fog imaginable, seeing herself as the heroine of the hour. When my grandfather returned the next day, instead of being proud of her achievement, he was absolutely furious with his daughter for driving with no licence or insurance. The tabloids would have a field day with such a story today.

Both my maternal grandparents had a wonderful sense of humour, a sense of fun that quite literally accompanied them to the grave. Grandfather Scott died in 1944, and his funeral was followed by burial in the churchyard at Kings Worthy in Hampshire, where they lived. The funeral procession duly arrived by the graveside, where the undertakers discovered they had made a monumental blunder. As they prepared to lower the coffin into the freshly dug grave, they realized they didn't have sufficient rope. Dare they risk just dropping him in? To the rescue came Grandfather's gamekeeper, a rotund, red-faced gentleman by the name of Fisk, who to everyone's amazement stripped off his jacket and removed his braces, motioning to me to do the same. I was only thirteen, but I knew an emergency when I saw one, and I shed my own braces with alacrity. With two sets of sturdy elasticated supports securely wrapped around his coffin, Grandfather was lowered into his final resting place with a degree of dignity. My mother said afterwards that he would have relished the drama, and fortunately my grandmother Scott saw the funny side of it too.

When Granny Scott died in 1948, she was cremated, and her ashes were to be buried alongside my grandfather. I was detailed to collect the ashes from the crematorium by car and take them on to the churchyard.

'She would have loved that final journey to King's Worthy,' said Mother afterwards. 'It was just what she would have wanted – to be wrapped in a brown paper parcel, in the back of the car, with Ronald's dogs jumping all over her!'

One of my earliest memories of Grandfather Ferguson was an accident with his wheelchair. It was electric, and terribly newfangled for its day. Once my mother even took it to the local railway station to collect my aunt who had been away for the weekend. 'Where's the car, where's the car?' my aunt cried in horror when she saw it.

As a small boy, I was entranced by this wheelchair. I used to sit in the front with my grandfather, studying its various mechanical details, as together we drove slowly round his garden. One afternoon, when Grandfather was having a sleep, I decided to take the chair out for a spin. In those days wheelchairs were battery-powered, and a knob on the side controlled the speed, with settings of one to four. Four was the fastest, at which point there was a stop mechanism in the form of a notch. I thought I'd be clever and that if I pushed the knob past the notch, I would go faster. But I couldn't get the knob back again, so there I was, hurtling round the garden completely out of control. The wheelchair flew faster and faster, tore across the manicured Polebrooke lawn and splashed straight into the ornamental lake, sending the ducks and swans squawking for their lives. For the first time in my life (certainly not the last), I was in big trouble.

My mother tells me I was a naughty little boy, in contrast to my brother John, who was tidy, punctual and perfect. To local people I was known as the Baby Ogre for I was apparently a nightmare at parties, breaking up toys and generally creating chaos. There are some who would say that not much has changed!

I've ridden horses all my life. There's a picture of me at the age of two strapped into a basket saddle on my first pony, a Shetland called Flying Flash. Mother says that when she began to teach me to ride a horse, I was the most obstinate child she had ever come across. Both my parents were very accomplished riders, and as well as being taught by them, I was also taken out on a leading rein with George Gilson, the huntsman of the Warwickshire.

Schooldays began at a small but apparently exclusive establishment known as Miss Dennison's. Mother often caused quite a stir by driving us there in a pony and cart. It would seem that mothers then were just as competitive as they are now. One of them asked my mother one day, 'Have you had this term's report? What did it say about Ronald?'

'Trying,' Mother said. 'I think that's marvellous because he is so lazy.' Next term, the same mother was upset because her son had received a bad report. 'Have you had yours? What did it say?' she asked. My mother still recalls her reply. 'It said, "Very trying".' That other small boy with the bad report went on to become Lord Lieutenant of Warwickshire.

Those early years are crystallized in my memory as being perfect, happy and sunny, despite the threat of an impending war in Europe. When John left Miss Dennison's for his prep school, Summerfields, in Oxford, he was put straight into the first cricket XI; he was a natural at sport. Then, in 1939, a dark cloud descended on my family which had nothing to do with Britain declaring war on Germany. John, aged only ten, was taken seriously ill and died of nephritis, a kidney infection for which there was then no cure. My mother has never quite got over it, and she says it almost killed my father, who was very close to John.

After John's tragic death, Mother had to pick up the pieces alone, since my father was serving in the Middle East with his regiment. She was determined that I wasn't to be brought up an only child, and resolved to live nearer her parents, at Kings Worthy, between Dummer and Winchester. So in 1941 we moved from Warwickshire to a rented house, the Dower House, Crawley, where we stayed for about six months. During this time, I went off to board at Ludgrove School, near Wokingham, and Mother and her friends hunted around for a house to buy in Hampshire. She heard that Dummer House, in the village of Dummer, near Basingstoke, was up for sale at a rock-bottom price; the owner had all his money tied up in some London flats which had been bombed. Mother bought Dummer House in 1942, without my father ever having seen it, and moved in with her sister Patricia and seven children, of whom only one was her own.

Mother's sister Patricia had a particularly tragic war. She was first married to Douglas Faulkner who commanded the Irish Guards. He was killed at Narvik, drowned as a result of a direct hit, in which many senior officers perished. She had two children by him, David and Hermione Faulkner. Patricia then married Douglas Faulkner's best friend, David Scrimgeour Wedderburn of the Scots Guards, and they had two daughters, Elizabeth and Janet. Tragically, David was to lose his life at Anzio, and my aunt, already widowed once by the war, heard of the loss of her second husband over the telephone when she was playing cards at Dummer House. Patricia subsequently married David's brother Jim, who inherited the title of the Earl of Dundee; their son Alexander is the present Earl. On this third marriage, Patricia took her younger daughters to live with her in Fife, but David and Hermione remained at Dummer. We also had living with us my cousins Ann and Sarah, whose mother Susan, Father's sister, had died of endocarditis in 1939. Here, too, is another connection with the Life Guards; Ann and Sarah's father was Lieutenant Colonel F.E.B. 'Boy' Wignall who commanded the Life Guards between 1943 and 1946.

Dummer House is a fine Georgian building of cream-coloured stone that once belonged to King George IV. He used it as his hunting box. The story goes that one of the King's mistresses, Mrs Kilpatrick, had lived in Kempshott House, which has since been demolished, about a mile away across the fields. It must have been quite a convenient arrangement, particularly as in those days there were no tabloid newspapers or paparazzi with long-lensed cameras to shout the liaison to the world.

During the war years, Dummer House was a riot of children. It had nine bedrooms and a glorious garden, ideal for us to tear about in and explore. I remember clearly David Faulkner and I towing my cousin Hermione on her tricycle until she fell off. The more we towed, the faster we went, and the more she cried. She told my mother recently that she had loved every minute of these small torments we devised.

Mother ran a YMCA canteen. In the holidays I was allowed to hand out sticky buns and pour the tea from the urns, taking great care not to slop it all over Mother's feet, or I'd be in trouble once more. Mother and I always had a close relationship, which remains to this day. When I was recovering from whooping cough, she took me to Minehead in a little black Ford. Its engine was far too feeble to tackle the hill into Minehead, but Mother, resourceful as ever, found a way. She simply reversed the car and went up backwards.

During the war my father was away a great deal with his regiment in the Middle East. He was a real hero to me – six foot three, with sandy brown hair, he looked really distinguished in uniform. I remember the thrill of seeing him when he came home on a short leave, wearing drab khaki, which seemed to me the most glamorous outfit imaginable. He would take me to the cinema in London, or, even more excitingly, to lunch at the Causerie in Claridges.

Father had been born left-handed, which my grandfather considered an aberration, so he was forced to become right-handed. As a result, he developed a stammer which he retained all his life. At one stage it nearly stopped him being given a commission in the Army. He was patient, kind and firm, a quiet person who enjoyed his own company. He was a beautiful horseman and taught me to have soft hands and to use my legs, instead of my hands, to stay on and to stop the horse. Later these skills stood me in good stead on the polo field.

Father had the most marvellous dry sense of humour. Once, for instance, Mother had spent hours arranging flowers for guests who were coming for the weekend. Father took them all away, leaving just one flower in each pot. He was an extraordinary mix of character. Although shy, at a royal occasion, for instance, Father would often be the first to get up and ask the Queen to dance. He was a tremendous companion, and I particularly loved going with him to the races. He had an almost encyclopedic knowledge of the sport, and even enjoyed a little light gambling. In the hunting field, he much preferred to ride off on his own; you'd often find him on the top of a hill, well away from the rest of the field.

He loved to shoot, and on a shooting day, rather than coming back to the dining room for lunch, he would make his guests have sandwiches and a bottle of beer under a haystack. Rather like his hunting, after a drive on his own farm, he would vanish. You didn't see him for the next two drives. Then he would turn up in the middle of a drive with his dog and there would be total chaos. He had a series of spaniels that managed to upset most shoots in Hampshire.

He loved animals and was especially fond of dogs, but however well trained they were when he acquired them, they soon got out of control. He was too kind to them, and wouldn't discipline them.

My father was often unpredictable. In fact, once you knew him, you expected it, thus he became predictable. There was a story that the officers in his regiment were ordered to do a special exercise in the desert at a specific time. To their amazement, they saw him coming back before they had set off, having decided to do the exercise by himself and not to bother his fellow officers with it.

He had been a seven-goal polo player before the war, but afterwards he never played again, preferring instead to umpire. On one occasion, Prince Philip was shouting and becoming more and more irate both with the players and with his own horse. 'Carry on like that, and you'll be sent off,' Father warned. Prince Philip, who is used to getting his own way, was astonished and duly reported this incident to Col. Gerard Leigh, then chairman of the Guards Polo Club. The end result was that Father was never invited to umpire again, which he thought was pathetic on the part of the authorities.

My mother said he was extremely proud of me when I first started to play polo, although you would never believe this. Father got a great deal of pleasure himself out of playing polo, but he appeared at the beginning to do everything he could to sabotage my game. He would come to every single match, but it was my mother who made sure that I had a horse to ride. He was exactly the same when I rode in point-to-points. It was as if he first had to establish that you really wanted to do something. Once he was convinced there was a commitment, he would get right behind you and be terribly encouraging. He was a wonderful man, but in many ways he was restless: whatever he was doing, he always wished he was doing something else.

I'm sure I was a disappointment to him when I had to leave Eton prematurely (of which more later), and afterwards when I failed the Army promotion exams. He knew then that I would never take command of the Life Guards, as he had. But if he was disappointed, he never showed it. Instead, he was always encouraging, making plans for me to have extra tuition so I could pass. I know he was pleased when I became Adjutant of the Life Guards before going to Aden in 1958, and also when I later became Squadron Leader with both the Mounted Regiment and the Armoured Car Regiment. While I was away on military duties, he was very supportive to my first wife Susie, and he adored his grandchildren Jane and Sarah. He was a great organizer, a tremendous man-manager, and respected by all ranks in the Household Cavalry during and after the war.

From the moment he had his first stroke, brought on by leukaemia, he tried terribly hard to disguise the fact that he was a semi-invalid. He loved being at Dummer Down, the smaller house on the estate where he and Mother had moved during his illness. Mother had roped the stairs so he could get up and down more easily. One day, a lunch guest, noticing the strange ropes on the stairs, commented, 'I see you've got dry rot too.'

'Dry rot?' snorted my father. 'The only thing that's got dry rot around here is me.'

It was agony for me to see this once proud man physically deteriorate before my eyes. Eventually he went into a nursing home in Sarum Road, Winchester. I took time off from my duties at every opportunity to be with him, and to help my mother. In August 1966, it was announced in *The Times* that I was to play polo for England in the Argentine that following autumn. I read it out to him, for by then he could no longer read, and he was thrilled, after all the support he had given me in taking up polo. He died two days later, and I still miss him enormously.

I was glad that my mother was able to find happiness again later. In 1968 she married Air Marshal Sir Thomas Elmhirst, a widower who was several years older than she, with a distinguished war record. A small man with big bushy eyebrows, and a fiery temper, he loved to fish and shoot, and had an expert knowledge of trees. We got on well together, and he was tremendously helpful with advice about trees on the estate. They lived in the village in Dummer and were happy together until, sadly, he died of a stroke in 1976.

My mother, although lame with a bad hip, is healthy at the age of eighty-six. She is mentally alert, drives herself everywhere, and treats me like a sixteen-year-old.

CHAPTER TWO

All Sport and No Work

IN THE AUTUMN of 1942, at the age of ten, I went to Ludgrove Preparatory School. My father and his brother Victor were former pupils, and in time my own son Andrew would attend the same school. Set in grounds of three hundred acres near Wokingham in the lush Berkshire countryside, Ludgrove had both an excellent academic record and superb sporting facilities. I should have gone there at the normal age of eight, but it was wartime and many unusual things were going on around us.

Ludgrove's headmaster was Alan Barber, who had been a triple blue at Oxford, played cricket for Yorkshire, and had captained the England touring side. Not surprisingly, he was to be an enormous influence on my sporting activities. To a small boy who was fast developing a passion for sport, Ludgrove was paradise – cricket, football, fives, squash, gymnastics . . . and lots of it. Looking back, I can see that the educational rot set in at Ludgrove – not because the school failed me, but because I became so caught up in sport that I managed to sidestep the work, which I hated anyway.

On Sunday nights, Mrs Barber held something called 'Mrs Barber's Reading'; this involved the whole school sitting on the floor in the drawing room listening to extracts from literature intended to improve our minds, but which more often numbed our senses. The evening began with a noisy scramble for the best places on the floor. Getting behind the large sofa was held at a premium, for it meant that, safely hidden, you could talk, laugh and play games, and totally ignore Mrs Barber's perorations.

Once, having overestimated the security of the sofa, I was sent out in disgrace and soundly beaten by Alan Barber. My partner in crime, who was also beaten, was Ronald Cunningham Jardine, who is now Lord Lieutenant of Dumfries in Scotland. Beating was a normal punishment, and when Alan beat us, it hurt. I would never lay a hand on my own children, but I believe beating never did me any harm. Besides, Ludgrove fielded a much worse punishment. Our gymnastics instructor, Sergeant Major Goldy – a very good instructor but a hard man – had devised something called Extra Drill. Miscreants were forced to perform a series of complicated exercises in the gym, carrying a phenomenally antiquated rifle that weighed a ton. Unlike a beating, whose after effects were minimal, an Extra Drill session caused you to suffer for days.

Petrol was severely rationed in wartime, which meant that Mother wasn't always able to drive over to see me at weekends. We met in Reading instead; my cousin David Faulkner and I would ride our bicycles to Wokingham station and take the train. Our mothers would travel by train from Basingstoke and we'd all meet up at the Great Western Hotel for lunch. This was a great treat for me, and must have meant a good deal to my mother; it was only a few years since John had died, and my father was serving with his regiment in the Middle East.

I just scraped the common entrance examination for Eton, passing in at the lowest level possible. I know I'd never pass it today. I thought I could get through by playing a lot of games and doing the minimum amount of work. I was lucky.

Eton College is a fantastic school, an establishment which allows you to pursue your own interests. My interest remained sport and I pursued it single-mindedly. Academic work was a different story. I never concentrated fully in class, and did as little as I could get away with outside. As a result, I lived in constant fear of failing exams. I benefited from only a fraction of what Eton had to offer. I regret this wasted opportunity but it was entirely my fault.

Eton had its own set of examinations, called Trials, taken in the summer half and again before Christmas. I managed to fail Trials twice. To join the army I also had to pass the army exam. Obviously I wasn't going to do that from Eton, so I was sent off to a crammer at Bishop's Waltham in Hampshire. I felt utterly devastated. However, it wasn't all work. I was allowed to have a horse at the local stable and hunted regularly with the Hambledon, as well as playing cricket for the local Bishop's Waltham team. But the time spent there was productive as well as formative, for eventually I passed the dreaded army exam and was able to follow in the footsteps of my father, grandfather and great-grandfather. In September 1949, one month before my eighteenth birthday, I became the fourth generation of Fergusons to join the Life Guards, as a trooper at Combermere Barracks, Windsor.

After Combermere, we were sent to the Brigade Squad at Caterham Barracks. This was a tough course with a massive amount of drill. From Caterham, I went to the Mons Officer Cadet School, then joined the main Military Academy at Sandhurst in September 1950. My Company Commander, Major W.G. (Legs) Lyon, was a keen cricketer, which made life easier for me during the summer of 1951 when I joined the cricket XI. The Company Sergeant Major, Les Cullen, was a delightful man – more like a nanny than the average CSM, but woe betide you if you ever let him down. He wasn't a shouter – this honour belonged to the legendary Jack Lord, then Regimental Sergeant Major at Sandhurst. We were terrified of him. He had incredible eyesight and could spot you slouching on parade from a thousand yards, and his voice could certainly carry that far.

My educational progress at Sandhurst took the same route it had taken everywhere else – playing lots of sport and doing very little work. In my intermediate term, I became one of the Commandant's four Stick Orderlies, a great honour. The onerous duties this imposed were performed every other Sunday. First, we enjoyed an excellent breakfast with the Commandant, the late Major General David Dawnay and his wife Lady Katherine, then we preceded him to church.

We spent a good deal of time in my friend Trevor Dawson's Riley, driving up to London as fast as we could. At nineteen, I was firmly fixed on the débutantes' lists of bright (or in my case, not so bright) young men. Endless invitations to parties and dances were on offer, and frequently we only just made it back to Sandhurst by the following BRC (Breakfast Roll Call). Trevor was a good but fast driver. He used to terrify us, reaching speeds of well over 70 m.p.h. – breathtakingly fast for those days – as we tore through the dawn down the A4.

I first began to ride in point-to-points at Sandhurst. During Christmas 1951 General Dawnay kindly loaned me his horse to use with the Hampshire Hunt. His son, Hugh, was at Sandhurst with me; he and I were later to become friendly rivals at point-to-points and on the polo field. Today Hugh Dawnay is probably the finest polo instructor in the world.

Point-to-pointing was regarded by the Sandhurst authorities as a character-building sport, but I needed little encouragement. These steeplechases, of approximately three and a half miles over fences slightly smaller than those used for National Hunt events, are fast, furious and occasionally extremely dangerous. To ride in point-to-points regularly I needed my own horse. My father wouldn't buy me one; his attitude, as usual, was never to encourage me to do anything until he was convinced I was serious about it. So Mother and I came up with a devious scheme. We found a horse called Numero Uno, owned by Harry Trigg. Unbeknown to my father, my mother bought it, but we left the horse where it was, and it continued to run in Harry's name. To the end of his days my father always wondered why this man Harry Trigg was so foolish as to allow me regularly to ride his horse. Eventually Father relented and bought me Cardinal's Drum, and I had a limited amount of success with him.

With the encouragement of Legs Lyon, and also Les Alderman, the Sandhurst coach who had played for Derbyshire, I developed my cricketing skills quite quickly. In the summer of 1951, I was thrilled to play in a match for the Royal Military Academy against the MCC at Lord's – the first and last occasion I played on this historic ground. As at school, being successful at sport made a huge difference to your standing at Sandhurst. While it was obvious that my academic results were going to be pathetic, my sporting achievements tipped the balance in my favour when it came to assessing my final passing-out grade. It was probably far higher than I deserved.

When I did pass out, in February 1952, I was one of the only Sandhurst intake who didn't take part in a proper parade, with all its pomp and circumstance. King George VI had died on 6 February, and our parade was cancelled as a mark of respect. We were bitterly disappointed. We had done all the rehearsals, and were really looking forward to marching up the great steps at Sandhurst and through the main doors, accompanied by the band playing 'Auld Lang Syne'. As a small boy, I had been awed by the sight of my father in his uniform; now I longed to be part of the splendour and tradition of a grand ceremonial parade.

CHAPTER THREE

Army Days – and Nights

AFTER LEAVING Sandhurst I went to Bovington Camp in Dorset. Then in May 1952 came my first posting abroad, to Wolfenbuttl near Hanover in Germany. I was now a second lieutenant and I joined A Squadron, which was to remain my squadron for the rest of my army career.

Soon after arriving at Wolfenbuttl, I was given an armoured car troop. My commanding officer in Germany was Colonel E.J.S. Ward, who would become Silver Stick to Her Majesty the Queen. Later he handed over command to Colonel W.H. Gerard Leigh, known as G., and thus began an association which was to last for over forty years both in the Army and on the polo field.

Life in Germany was great. In addition to a good deal of soldiering there were horse shows, point-to-points and hunter trials to ride in. Social life consisted of numerous parties between the various regiments, and periodically each would have a dance or a ball following a point-to-point or a horse show. We were allowed to invite girls out from England to be our escorts at these functions. I persuaded one girlfriend to come out and join me for a party, someone I'd taken out back home – we had been to the theatre and held hands a lot. She was a pretty, petite brunette of about eighteen. She stayed in married quarters. The girls were supposed to be chaperoned, but they rarely were – you had about as much freedom as you would have had staying in someone's house at home, which wasn't much. In the prim early fifties free love wasn't on the agenda. Kissing and cuddling and trying to take liberties was as far as you went. Going to bed with a girlfriend wasn't even talked and joked about in the Mess – all that came later.

Before long, Second Lieutenant Ferguson had found yet another sporting challenge which could pre-empt doing anything more intellectually taxing. I had learned to ski on winter holidays as a child, so as soon as the snow arrived a group of us went off to the mountains at Bad Harzburg. This was not a leisure pursuit, but practice training prior to going to Kitzbühel to train more seriously for the Army Ski Championships in Bad Gastein, Austria. We had a private instructor who got us up at the crack of dawn and made us ski very hard. We were already fit when we got there, but we soon got even fitter.

The Army Ski Championships of 1952/3 were to be my first and last attempt to race, although I didn't know it at the time. The main event was the downhill. Predictably this was the favourite among the young blades – we fancied ourselves no end hurtling down the mountain. We had to get through the slalom first, which none of us was particularly good at. On one occasion Ferguson managed to catch a ski tip on a slalom pole on the lower slopes, and hit the ground hard. I was so disappointed that I let forth several four-letter words in frustration. Standing a few yards away was the Army Commander in Germany, accompanied by his wife and prim teenage daughter. (We knew, from experience, that the daughter was, indeed, *very* prim.) I pulled myself up and skied on down the slope, thinking no more of it. But on returning to my regiment after the championships, I discovered that the General had written a letter to my commanding officer. 'In future,' he suggested, 'it would be preferable to select officers for the ski team who do not swear when they fall over.'

Final practice day for the downhill loomed. My start time was in the late afternoon, when the sun had softened the surface of the snow, so the going was relatively slow. After the first 250 yards the course turned sharp right through some trees. That afternoon all of us judged the turn perfectly and made good times. In the evening we didn't go out, such was our anticipation of the big race that lay ahead.

My start time was 10.15 a.m., when conditions on the piste were completely different. It was cold, the snow was still frozen, and the going would be much faster. I hadn't appreciated just how much faster; I completely misjudged that first right-angled corner, took it much too quickly, and slammed straight into a tree. It knocked me unconscious – no time to swear – and I was out for ten days, waking up in hospital with a fairly bad headache. That was the end of my racing career. The rest of the team went back to Wolfenbuttl, and I returned, discharged with warnings from the hospital.

Shortly after that, Colonel Gerard Leigh decided that I would be a suitable candidate for the PT course at Aldershot. This was often regarded as punishment – officers who had done something terrible, or who had behaved badly, were shunted there. But Colonel Gerard Leigh knew that I was keen to ride in point-to-points and that sport was never a punishment to me. Aldershot was a bonus.

The course was tough and I loved it. My room-mate in the Officers' Mess was Captain Michael 'Docker' Boyle of the Irish Guards. Docker was the most unsuitable person for a PT course. We all felt sorry for him. He wasn't remotely athletic and couldn't do half the things he was asked to do. He couldn't cope with army food either, so three times a week a hamper from Fortnum & Mason would arrive. Docker, being a generous chap, would share its contents with the rest of us. He was a lovable character and in view of this – and those Fortnum & Mason delicacies – we all covered for him. The poor chap went through hell, but instead of being sent back to his unit, he succeeded in passing-out with the rest of us.

Riding in a point-to-point in Sussex in the spring of 1953, I had a spectacular accident. I was in the lead, but fell at a fence and landed on my back. As the rest of the field galloped over me, one horse thoughtfully placed his foot flat on my chest, at the spot where, unknown to me, I'd already broken my right collarbone. The pain was excruciating. The fence was way out in the country. The first-aid people not only had difficulty reaching me; they promptly dropped both me and the stretcher on the way back to the ambulance. It's an experience I never want to repeat.

This broken collarbone posed other problems. If the military authorities had known about it, they would never have allowed me to march with my regiment in the forthcoming Coronation of Queen Elizabeth II on 7 June. I had no choice but to grin and bear it. We marched in tight overall trousers, which were braced up tightly underneath our tunics, the straps passing over the collarbone. We began our march from Earls Court barracks at 4.30 a.m., with thundering hangovers caused by anticipating the celebrations a little too vigorously the night before. For the first few hours, I kept my right braces deliberately loose, creating an interesting concertina effect in my right trouser leg. Later I tightened the braces and gritted my teeth, determined not to allow the pain to take over. We marched along the Coronation route to our forming-up position at the bottom of St James's Street, near where Prunier's restaurant used to be. There, our lunch arrived in haversacks. In the balconies above the street were some acquaintances of my friend Ian Baillie, who was marching alongside me. They kindly threw him down a bread roll to supplement the rations. Ian decided he didn't want it, so he speared the bread roll neatly on the end of his ceremonial sword and flicked it back onto the balcony in one breathtakingly accurate movement.

While the service was taking place, thousands of men from all the armed services were lined up along the route, waiting for the long ceremony to finish. At a given signal, when the

Coronation coach moved off, we too moved off as one and proceeded along the route, marching back up St James's, along Piccadilly and Park Lane to Marble Arch and eventually back to our barracks at Earls Court – a twelve-hour day of marching. Christopher Philipson, whom I'd met in Germany, John Gooch and I were sharing a flat at 27, The Boltons, South Kensington. By the time we got back, my collarbone was agony, but worse, we had to cut John Gooch's boots off. There were pools of blood where they had chafed his heels raw, though we hadn't heard a murmur of complaint from him all day.

In 1954 our regiment was sent to the Canal Zone in Egypt. Much to our delight, also on board ship was a party of nurses. We spent most of our time plotting devious ways of meeting them, while contriving to escape the attentions of the older, less attractive nursing officers, who were keeping a strict eye on their young charges. Christopher Philipson and I later invited a number of them to come and see us at the Officers' Club at Fanara. This led to the Officers' Club writing a sharp letter to the hospital matron saying could they please make sure the nurses no longer used the club. They were banned because they weren't officers, which we thought was terribly stuffy. We had offended army etiquette; older officer nurses were welcome, pretty young ones were not.

The accommodation at Fanara camp comprised large tents with sparse, basic furniture – wardrobes, chairs, beds, matting on the floor, and no hot or cold water. You shaved and washed in a communal tin hut washroom, or used an old-fashioned commode. From time to time, local inhabitants would cut through the wires and burrow into the camp at night to do some petty pilfering. I woke up one night to see someone in my tent – a boy of about sixteen. I leaped up and flew out of the tent after him. Unfortunately I was wearing only pyjama bottoms and the cord came undone. The pyjamas dropped to the ground, tripped me up and I plummeted headfirst into the sand. Some would say this was not the only time I've been caught with my trousers down. The thief was never apprehended.

Before going out to the Canal Zone, I'd been seeing a girl in London I'd grown fond of. The night before I left, we went together to see a production of *Swan Lake*. I was so entranced with the music that I bought the complete set of records and played them constantly in Egypt. My fellow officers became so fed up with macho young Ferguson listening rapt to Tchaikovsky at full volume, day and night, that they threatened to destroy the records unless I stopped. To this day I only have to hear the opening bars of the overture, and I'm instantly transported back to Egypt.

Although there was no fighting, an enormous amount of military work had to be done. We were there to keep the peace. It was a challenge to learn how to navigate over desert terrain, without roads or tracks, either by using a compass or the stars for guidance. I came to enjoy the desert as much as my father had during the war.

I vividly remember a night exercise when the whole of the division transport had to move through mountain passes to a rendezvous by dawn. I was selected to lead Division HQ vehicles. There was no chance to recce the area in advance as we were pretending it was wartime, but, as an arrogant young officer all of twenty-two years of age, I had every confidence in what I considered to be my excellent map-reading skills. We set off at 11 p.m., leading a convoy of about three hundred assorted vehicles, with no lights on. After about two hours of driving I discovered that the pass I had believed was the correct one came to a grinding halt. It was far too narrow to proceed. By this time the entire convoy was in the pass and the only way was back. It was too narrow to turn the vehicles round. So, in the middle of the night, with no lights to guide us, Land-rovers, three-tonners, one-tonners, petrol vehicles, cooks' wagons, the lot, all had to be reversed back up the pass. The chaos was unbelievable. The cry went: 'Left hand down a bit. Right hand down a bit. Steady.' Then *crunch* as a vehicle ran into the side of the pass, or the vehicle behind it. The Divisional Commander wasn't best pleased.

Romance blossomed in Egypt too. I was taking out a secretary who was attached to SIME (Special Investigation Middle East), and became quite involved with her. My commanding officer Colonel Gerard Leigh evidently thought I was seeing too much of her, so he consulted with my father and Colonel Ward, who was then Silver Stick to the Household Cavalry. Colonel Ward sent a message back: 'Do you consider it necessary for Ferguson to be returned to England?' I know, because I saw the message. The adjutant who should have received it was on leave. As his assistant, it came first to me. Under normal circumstances, it was my duty to show it to my commanding officer. Instead, I sent a message back: 'Not necessary Ferguson return to England,' and signed it 'G'. It was never referred to again, and for years I didn't tell anyone about this unauthorized interception.

From time to time, to our delight, hospitals in Alexandria used to hold Red Cross balls. Dancing partners were at a premium, so the Divisional Commander was detailed to send a number of officers to escort the nurses to these functions. The demand for tickets was enormous, but Christopher Philipson and I soon devised ways of getting to the front of the queue! We'd travel to Alexandria by train, quite an experience in itself, stay in private houses as guests, and all join up for the dinner dance, looking frightfully glamorous in our Mess kit of short jackets, tight overall trousers and spurs.

In the Canal Zone, one of the more immediate problems was finding private transport to enable us to carry on our social lives. We bought a Straight 8 Packard in moderate condition and decided to give it a facelift. Sleek shiny black was our original choice, but as soon as we put on the first coat of paint, a sandstorm blew up and the car ended up a gritty grey, rather like a mobile nail file. Getting spare parts for the Packard presented another challenge. One item was available only at the Packard HQ in West London. After many signals, telephone calls and messages, it was finally located and sent out through the Naafi – nothing was too much trouble for that car! She guzzled petrol, but we were fortunate that Christopher was the signals officer. The battery charger, which was used to keep all the wireless batteries topped up, was petrol driven. Never in the history of telecommunications has one petrol-driven battery charger used so much fuel.

Although my father had been a seven-goal player before the Second World War, as a boy I had never been taken to watch a polo match. I'd heard and read much about it, including the famous Rudyard Kipling story, 'The Maltese Cat', about a polo player in India. I was entranced by the idea of this exciting game which seemed to combine two of the greatest joys in my life – playing sport and riding horses. In Egypt, in 1954, Colonel Gerard Leigh made it clear that he wanted me to play and he was very encouraging. I started by practising on the regiment's polo ponies – about fourteen were stabled at the barracks at Fayed – and I remember writing proudly back to my father, 'Wonderful practice session today. I dribbled the ball the whole length of the field.' His reply was less than enthusiastic: 'You've nothing to be proud of. Polo is a team game. You should have passed the ball on to somebody else and got yourself into a position to receive the pass back.' Undaunted, I continued to practise, and was soon detailed to be part of the team taking the polo ponies to Cairo for a match between the British Army and the Egyptian Police at the fabulous Gezira Sporting Club, which had three polo grounds of its own.

On the morning of the match, Colonel Gerard Leigh received a message to say that one of the team members was ill. A totally inexperienced substitute, I was asked to step in. When the opposing team arrived our hearts sank. Their horses were much bigger than our small Arab Barbs, genuine thoroughbreds which completely outclassed ours. It was a hot and sunny day, and crowds poured into the Sporting Club in their hundreds, for this was the first time for years that there had been a polo match between the British and the Egyptians. On one side of the ground a complete *Who's Who* of Cairo was lined up, the ladies smartly attired in their summer hats and matching parasols. On the other, crammed tightly into the stands with barely room to move, was a huge crowd of locals brightly clad in colourful djellabahs, waving and shouting their pleasure and enthusiasm.

It was clear from the first chukka that we were going to be completely slaughtered. The Egyptian Police team was experienced. They not only hit the ball harder and more accurately than we did, they also positioned themselves better. By half-time in this six chukka match, we were twenty goals down. After every chukka, an army of groundsmen swarmed onto the grass and set to work to put what seemed like even the smallest blade back into position. It was like playing on a billiard table. In forty years, I've never played on a ground that was maintained in such immaculate condition. Although I didn't play well, I managed to hit the ball, though not always straight! By half-time, I was exhausted. The following day, to our surprise and pleasure, our horses trotted out sound, despite the rigours of the previous match. We had the same, even bigger crowds and this time we improved our performance by 200 per cent, ending with a final score of 32–2.

That evening, having showered and changed, the Egyptians gave a tremendous reception for us at the Gezira Club. The way they handed out the prizes, you would have been forgiven for thinking that both matches were desperately close, and that the Egyptian Police had only just managed to win.

'Sell my point-to-point horses,' I wrote to my father. 'When I get back to England, I'm only going to play polo.'

CHAPTER FOUR

Marriage and Fatherhood

LONDON FOR ME in 1955 was a hectic whirl of military duties at Hyde Park Barracks by day, playing as much polo as I could in my time off, and enjoying a non-stop social life by night. I was intent on burning the candle at both ends and in the middle too as long as the energy lasted – and that was just on weekdays! I shared a flat, and many adventures, with Christopher Philipson in Melbury Road, off Kensington High Street. As a subaltern in the Life Guards, I participated in all the great State occasions such as Trooping the Colour, State visits, the opening of Parliament. As young serving officers, we were much in demand for balls and parties, and during the Season, the invitations came thick and fast.

I spent weekends at home in Dummer, riding in local point-to-points and catching up with friends. We'd go to each other's houses for dancing and perhaps a buffet supper. There were no discos – we'd put on the records, turn out the lights and hope for the best. Sex before marriage was still out of bounds, but that didn't stop us trying our luck. In the mid-fifties you didn't limit yourself to one girlfriend – you had several, juggling dates, times and places to keep them all on the go at the same time.

My friend, the late Mark Jeffreys, and I used to swap girlfriends about three times a year, amicably and with no discussion in advance. He had one girlfriend, however, whom we didn't swap. Frances Roche later became Frances Althorp, mother of the Princess of Wales, and many years later I was astonished to hear Viscount Althorp make the inaccurate statement on American television that I had once made a proposal of marriage to his mother.

I met my first wife Susie at a dance. She was then Susan Wright, the niece of Viscount Powerscourt. She was doing the débutante season at the tender age of seventeen, staying with various friends and relatives in London. I was attracted to her from the start. Susie was vivacious and lively, and she seemed to enjoy all the things that I enjoyed. She had a touch of Irish wildness about her, and she was a country girl, having been brought up in Lincolnshire and at her grandfather's castle in County Wicklow. It was a real fairytale castle, and was later the location for films such as *Excalibur* and *Camelot*. Susie won my heart because she enjoyed going to polo matches – an essential prerequisite for a Ferguson girlfriend in those days! – and she shared my love of horses and dogs. She was articulate, she was fun, she was a good companion – it seemed to me she had everything. My other girlfriends bit the dust as a result of her being on the scene.

Her mother, Doreen, known as Dar, was a wonderful character who remained a great friend of mine, and of my mother's, right up to her death in 1991 at the age of eighty-seven. However, back then in 1955, Susie's parents weren't at all sure she should marry so young, and hoped that by encouraging her to spend a few months in France learning the language, they would at least delay matters. There was nothing unusual in this; indeed, one day, I would send Jane to stay with friends abroad. Dar and Fitz, Susie's father, didn't send her away because they didn't like me – quite the opposite, in fact.

When Susie came back later in the summer it was a classic example of absence making the heart grow fonder. I cannot now remember how we decided to get married, whether I asked her in London, at her home, or at mine. Perhaps she even asked me. When we became engaged, Susie was just eighteen and I was approaching twenty-four. Susie has written in her memoirs that we were far too young; maybe that's true, but we were very happy together at the time.

Our wedding was held at St Margaret's, Westminster, in January 1956, and, like her grandfather's castle, it had a touch of the fairytale about it. For a start, it was colourful and grand. There were serving officers in both our families, so it was the done thing to have all the rigmarole, including the Guard of Honour. The reception was held at Claridges for six hundred guests, arranged by Susie's father who had business connections with the hotel.

For our honeymoon, we had planned to fly to Paris, to stay at the Hotel George V, and then take the train on to Austria for a skiing holiday in Kitzbühel. However, on the day of the wedding, Christopher Philipson, my best man, was told by the travel agent that Paris airport was fogbound. We had to think again very quickly. As we drove away from the reception at Claridges, only Christopher and I knew that we were going just a mile or so down the road to the Savoy Hotel. Our parents – and, indeed, Susie – still thought we were going to the airport!

The next morning we took the train to Austria from Victoria Station, a journey that will always be imprinted in my mind. I enjoyed the sleeper and the train, the noise and bustle, the French breakfast with croissants. It seemed that we were embarking on a huge adventure, and we felt terribly adult and excited. Susie had never skied, and, on reflection, maybe it wasn't the ideal location for a honeymoon, but in those days we knew nothing about winter sunshine and the West Indies, which is probably where one would go today.

Susie and I had our own ski guide; I'd ski with him in the mornings, then Susie would have tuition in the afternoons. During the day we only saw each other at lunchtime, although I'd hover around while she was having her lesson, or accompany her up the mountain when she went for a short run. This was the start of many happy skiing holidays, and later on we would take our daughters too.

Back home we settled in a flat in Chesham Place, Belgravia, which turned out to be slightly inconvenient as by now I had been transferred from Knightsbridge Barracks back to Combermere Barracks at Windsor. Transport was a problem; as a result of the Suez crisis petrol was rationed, but I wasn't keen to spend nights at Combermere when I could be with my new young bride in London. I acquired one of those ugly little cars, a Messerschmidt, with one wheel at the front and two at the back. It was most unsafe, but because of the petrol shortage, little traffic was on the roads.

Both our children were planned but there was too much pressure from would-be grandparents for us to delay for long. Everyone was delighted when our daughter Jane was born on 26 August 1957 at 27, Welbeck Street. I wasn't there for the birth – in those days, it was very rare for a father to be present. Susie had had a trouble-free pregnancy and I couldn't have cared less whether the baby was a boy or a girl. It made me laugh when my next daughter Sarah was born and people asked if I was disappointed not to have an heir. 'An heir to what?' I'd reply.

I must have tired of commuting, despite the Messerschmidt, because shortly after this we bought our first house, Lowood, in Ascot, where we lived until 1968. It was a lovely house, right opposite the Berystede Hotel, on a crossroads. About an hour's drive from London, it was a white Edwardian house with fourteen acres of garden and woodland, and a long drive up to the house lined with rhododendrons. With ten bedrooms and a tennis court, it seemed the perfect house for a growing family. These were happy days. We were a young couple who did many things together and shared the same interests, and the advent of a baby didn't curtail our lives, for we were fortunate in having a nanny. Susie wasn't a classic military wife; she had little to do with the army social life, but carried on with her own life and friends.

In the winter of 1957, our regiment was hoping for a posting to Hildesheim in Germany, where the married quarters were better than many in England. In March, however, we heard the largely unwelcome news that in the autumn we would be going on a tour to the Aden Protectorate, where married quarters were few and far between. I was devastated to be leaving my family behind but I had no choice. Little Jane was a few days short of her first birthday when I bade her and Susie a sad goodbye, not sure when I would see either of them again. I didn't know if it would be possible for Susie to come out to Aden. Our separation could last more than a year.

I was to sail with the regiment on the troopship *Dilwara* from Southampton, and, on the journey down from Combermere, I discovered that there would be a twenty-minute wait at Basingstoke station, where we would change trains. I alerted my mother and father and they and a crowd of Dummer villagers turned up and gave us a tremendous send-off. At Southampton it was the same story – hundreds of people came to wave us off, and the regimental band played on the quayside for two hours before the ship eventually sailed.

I was already a captain, and I was made up to adjutant when the previous incumbent was relieved of his duties following a fight with a fellow officer in the orderly room. I was thrown in at the deep end, taking over all the paperwork and organization involved in taking a whole regiment off to Aden.

The voyage took about a fortnight; the boat was old, the quarters cramped and inadequate. But it didn't take me long to find a diversion which involved sport and fresh air. Corporal of Horse Singleton and I discovered the delights of deck quoits. Aden was hot, arid, noisy, bustling – and I loved it. The *Dilwara* arrived on the evening of 3 September 1958, and it was decided not to dock until the following morning. The heat was so intense in the cabins of the now immobile ship that the officers spent that night sleeping on deck.

We were based at Little Aden, where BP had all their oil. The political situation there was complicated and our role was essentially a peace-keeping one. In addition to protecting the oil reserves in the area, there were skirmishes on the northern borders, which we had to guard, with Yemen so there was plenty of action. To my delight I was also able to play cricket three times a week. The wicket was of compo rubber, with an outfield of rolled sand, and we had some terrific matches with other regiments, with the RAF, and with the many other players from all nationalities who were out in the Gulf at the time. We swam within a huge shark net, went sailing, played football and even limited polo.

Football brought me back to England much sooner than I had expected. On Boxing Day 1958, I was playing in goal in a furious match against the NCOs' mess when I fell awkwardly and twisted a cartilage in my knee. I was flown back by RAF as a CASVAC (casualty evacuation) to Lyneham in Wiltshire to have the cartilage removed at the RAF hospital at Wroughton. This meant I would be reunited with Susie and Jane. Susie came to Lyneham to meet me and I remember the frustration when they made me travel to the hospital in the CASVAC bus – Susie had to follow behind in the car. She had arranged for me to have the operation done privately by Bill Tucker, an orthopaedic surgeon she knew who specialized in knee injuries. The RAF hospital wanted to do the operation there and then. 'Not on your life,' I said. Escaping the draconian matrons at RAF Wroughton was easier said than done and it took me a good six hours of wrangling to discharge myself from their clutches.

I had a couple of days at home with my family before the operation, and we hatched a plan to get Susie to return with me to Aden. I was dying to get back because I loved the life out there, but as it would take time for the knee to heal, it made sense to return by ship rather than plane. One of the serving officers' wives had good contacts with Shell, and Susie arranged for us to return to Aden on a 36,000-ton oil tanker. I could use the time as rehabilitation, and we could be together. Jane would be well looked after by her nanny and grandmother in Lincolnshire. Aden was certainly no place for a one-year-old baby, and this was by no means unusual then for army officers' children. Susie didn't seem to mind leaving Jane behind; there was never any question of her being coerced into it by me.

Making arrangements was one thing, getting on board quite another. I well remember struggling up the rope ladder to the tanker, dragging my left knee swathed in bandages. The sailing went smoothly until after the tanks had been emptied at Rotterdam prior to sailing through the Bay of Biscay. There we hit a storm that lasted six days. I'm a good sailor, but even I was suffering and poor Susie was pole-axed. Any fanciful notions we might have had about this being a second honeymoon went straight out of the porthole.

Once the storm died down, we found the trip thoroughly diverting. Being the only passengers on a tanker, we were able to spend a lot of time on the Captain's bridge learning about navigation. We had taken a good supply of books and we discovered one corner of the ship where sunbathing was possible. We enjoyed talking to the crew, learning something about other people's lives.

The voyage took three weeks, and included going down the spectacular Suez Canal, through the Bitter Lake and into the Red Sea. It was quite an adventure for us both. At Aden, we sent signals to the regiment, and they sent out an RAF launch to pick us up.

Much later, I was saddened to read in Susie's memoirs that she thought her time in Aden was hell. This was news to me –

she had wanted to join me and it was a great joy to have her there. We shared a house with another couple who did nothing but row, but we tried hard not to let it affect our lives – we just shut our ears! Life in Aden was completely different from anything we'd ever experienced before, it was hot and smelly and there wasn't any air conditioning, but there was plenty to learn, to do and see, and I thought we had a good time. Our second daughter Sarah was conceived in Aden, so Susie returned to England, again by ship, in the spring of 1959; I followed later on an RAF flight, after my regiment handed over duties to the Royals.

Like Jane, Sarah was born at 27, Welbeck Street, on 15 October 1959. A bright little baby with a shock of red hair, she brought me great joy. I was delighted to have two daughters, and as I was now back with the Life Guards at Combermere Barracks, I could at last spend time with my family. Whereas Jane had been a placid baby, Sarah certainly wasn't, and their personalities have never changed. They have remained chalk and cheese: Jane was tall and elegant, looked beautiful on a horse but didn't go fast, but while Sarah, too, looked good on horseback, although not as elegant as Jane, she rode flat out. It was the same when we taught the girls to ski: Jane was slim and stylish on skis, but progressed quite slowly; Sarah was dumpier and really went for it. Sarah tackles new tasks with obsessive energy and, on the whole, Jane takes things more cautiously. Those early years with them were some of the best in my life.

In late 1959, I was promoted to staff captain, London District on Horse Guards Parade. This was my first staff job away from the regiment, so I could get a broader picture of the regiments within the Household Division, and organize other people for events such as Trooping the Colour. By then I knew a great deal about ceremonial duties and I took pride in making sure that everything looked immaculate – the uniforms, the horses. The way a ceremonial occasion appeared was down to me and I had to impose impeccable standards, since the welfare of both men and horses was my responsibility. I loved producing a good squadron, and I know I achieved this, for it was confirmed when I went back for a second tour, something that has never happened before or since.

I was in charge of the churchyard at Bladon for Winston Churchill's funeral. Instead of being a tiny cog in a monster wheel in London, I was a much larger cog in a smaller wheel at Bladon, since on this occasion I had nothing to do with the ceremonial duties in London. Like all State funerals, it had been planned in advance right down to the smallest detail. Its codename was Operation Hopenot, and there are similar plans and other codenames laid down for all future State funerals, including those of the current Royal Family. As Churchill became progressively more ill, the file containing plans for his funeral was dragged out and dusted off, changes made and meetings called almost daily. We had a complete dress rehearsal for the funeral procession at Bladon. The hearse drew up outside the churchyard having first negotiated a narrow lane. For logistical reasons, the hearse then had to back up and drive away again before the bearer party could proceed. The driver had turned off the engine while the coffin was being removed. As the bearer party stood there, solemnly supporting the rehearsal coffin on their shoulders, the driver re-started the engine. The bearer party, the coffin, and the hearse were promptly engulfed in a dense billowing cloud of black smoke, as if the coffin had spontaneously combusted on the spot. As it was the rehearsal and not the real thing, it could almost be described as amusing.

'Produce another hearse,' I told the firm who were providing the cars. 'We can't allow this to happen on the day.'

Winston Churchill's funeral was the most solemn State occasion I have ever witnessed, with English weather to match – cold, grey, and threatening rain. I was conscious of the solemnity of the event, and the greatness of the man and what we owed him. I felt proud to be so closely involved and at the same time apprehensive. It was my responsibility to ensure that the military side went without a hitch. All went according to plan until the moment when the coffin, draped in its flag and bedecked with Winston Churchill's distinguished war and civilian medals, was about to be lowered into the grave. From my vantage point, I became aware that the officer who had been made responsible for removing the medals before the burial had forgotten his duties. The medals were about to go down with the coffin. A swift message to the officer in question averted that particular disaster.

Above, left: My grandfather, General Algernon Ferguson.

Above, right: My father, wearing his frock coat.

Right: Me looking dashing and rather smug.

Polebrooke Hall, near Oundle, the Ferguson family home.

Dummer House, my childhood home, where we moved in 1940.

My maternal grandmother, Margaret, at Polebrooke.

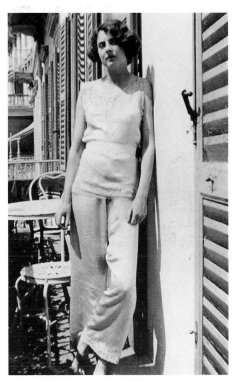

Auntie Pat (now Patricia, Countess of Dundee), my mother's sister.

My mother.

My parents' engagement photograph.

Grandpa Algie and me.

My father and fellow Life Guard officer Jack Speed.

Clockwise, from top left:

Me, aged two, looking remarkably like Sarah.

On holiday with brother John.

The beginning of a long riding career. I get better at it.

With John, a little more confident now.

Aged about thirteen, at Dummer House.

My first time in Life Guards uniform ...

... and son Andrew at Victor Law's wedding.

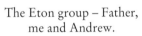

The Eton group – Father,
me and Andrew.

Stiff stick orderly at the Royal Military
Academy, Sandhurst.

On parade.

Before the Hambledon point-to-point where we came second. Thin and tense.

CHAPTER FIVE

A Life in Polo

MY FIRST SEASON of polo on home territory was at a private ground belonging to Archie David in Henley-upon-Thames. He must have been about seventy then, a great character with a deep and abiding love for the game. Archie had already invited Colonel Humphrey Guinness, a pre-war polo international, and Brigadier Andrew Horsburgh Porter, an experienced British Cavalry officer, to play for his team. They both did a lot to help me develop my game. As a novice player I started at a minus-two handicap. Within ten years, when I took part in a tour of the Argentine, it had risen to five goals. I was never as good as my father but I didn't feel I had to compete with his success. I just wanted to get as high a handicap as possible, and play as well as I could.

In 1956, the Household Brigade Polo Club (later to become the Guards Polo Club) was formed when Prince Philip decided that polo should be played on the ground at Smith's Lawn, an area formerly used as a landing strip. He gave instructions to the Duke of Wellington to make the necessary arrangements, and Archie David brought his horses over. Major General Claude Pert became Polo Manager, and Geoffrey Cross, chairman of the Royal Windsor Horse Show Club, Secretary. Claude was a pre-war polo international. He had spent many years with the Indian army and had a wonderful war record serving on Lord Mountbatten's staff. When he retired, my friend Willie Lloyd, with whom I had served in the Life Guards, took over as Polo Manager, and in 1971 I joined him as Deputy Chairman. We worked together for a decade. I was there five days a week in winter, seven in summer, and when Willie retired I decided it wasn't necessary to replace him. We just carried on.

The game of polo has done a lot for me, and from the minute I started playing I felt eager to give something back. Two ways of doing this were by umpiring and by helping players younger than myself. For twenty-two years, I was the chief umpire to the governing body of the game, the Hurlingham Polo Association. I like to think that I will be remembered for several things; innovations, such as striped shirts for umpires, starting games on time, improving facilities for spectators, and the standards of presentation, ensuring better maintenance of the grounds, and introducing charity matches.

Colonel Gerard Leigh's successor as Chairman, Colonel Richard Watt, had a less benign attitude towards me. During the years he was Treasurer, we had never really seen eye to eye, and it seemed that in my latter years he was keen to get rid of me. I was devastated when I left the Club in 1988. I had been there thirty-three years. My appointment as Deputy Chairman was voted for annually by the executive committee, but in 1988 I was not reappointed for 1989. Instead I was offered the position of running the polo, with no place on the executive committee, and with a chief executive above me. This was a totally unacceptable situation, which I declined. To this day, I feel sure that members were manipulated to vote me out. So many conflicting and erroneous rumours were flying about that, rarely for me, I issued a statement to the Press Association. I had already given Richard Watt the opportunity to make his own statement, but none was forthcoming. I sent him a copy of my statement. It said:

> To clear up any misunderstandings, I have not been sacked. I
> have not resigned. I was not re-elected as Deputy Chairman
> for 1988–89 and was not prepared to accept the alternative

position. I will be handing over my duties in October. I will continue to organize the Prince of Wales's polo matters and I will remain a life playing member of the Club. Having given a lifetime of devotion and dedication to the Guards Polo Club, I feel very sad and extremely angry at the way the whole matter has been handled.

I have never been told the true reason for my not being reappointed. I believe that Richard Watt no longer wished to be merely a figurehead. He wanted power, and while I was in place, it eluded him. Also, from the time that Sarah married into the Royal Family, I suspect he disliked the amount of media attention that was beamed on me (and indirectly, on the Club). He resented being less able to control me and he seemed jealous of any power or influence I might have.

In the spring of 1988, a report had been commissioned by the Club to ask the management consultants, Coopers and Lybrand, to look into the way it was run. When the consultant arrived, he spent roughly twenty minutes talking to me, but two-and-a-half days with the Chairman. Considering it was I who did the day-to-day running of the Club, this seemed odd, to say the least. I was amazed not to be consulted in more depth. When the report came out, a lot of the blame for the Club's unsatisfactory financial position was laid at my feet. I even heard, after I'd left, that there were rumours that I'd had my fingers in the till. Although I did authorize a great deal of money to be spent on the grounds, I could not have done anything dishonest since I never handled cash and had no authority to sign cheques. All that was done by the Chairman and the Honourable Treasurer. I am not a devious person – it would have been totally against my nature to have been involved in anything fraudulent. Perhaps I may be extravagant at times but, judging by the way the report was put together, I can only deduce that I was deliberately set up as the scapegoat.

I was deeply wounded by Prince Philip's refusal, as President of the Club, to discuss it with me. I made repeated requests to see him and appointments were made which were subsequently cancelled. Both the Prince of Wales and Sarah asked him if he would discuss it with me, but a deafening silence ensued. When I left, I was touched that many of the staff demonstrated their loyalty either by coming with me to the Royal Berkshire Polo Club, going to other positions, or pursuing other careers. Unprotected by me, many of them no longer wanted to work with the Chairman, whose management skills left a certain amount to be desired. The most upsetting aspect is that all the 'scandals' and tabloid trumpetings that went on about me or members of my family, seem to have eclipsed any contribution I have made to polo. This makes me very sad indeed. To the detriment sometimes of my family, friends and my farm, polo and the Guards Polo Club was my life – for nearly forty years.

At the end of the season in 1988, when it became clear that I was going to leave the Club, Bryan Morrison, Chairman of the Royal County of Berkshire Polo Club, and his partner, Norman Lobell, asked if I would like to join them as Director of Sponsorship. Bryan Morrison had been a friend of mine for years – before the Royal Berkshire opened, he had been a member of the Guards Polo Club and he and Norman had played there regularly. Bryan is a fiery, volatile character, a self-made millionaire who has plenty of ups and an abundance of downs, yet I like to think we understood each other well. The RCBPC had been in existence since 1985. Although it was already an established club, I knew that I would be able to help them gain a higher profile. As it turned out, the profile I finally did achieve for the Club was higher and a little more sensational than they originally envisaged!

My first day at work was 10 October 1988 – my fifty-seventh birthday – and as I drove through the gates of the Club, past the manicured lawns towards the sleek new architect-designed club-house, and entered my spacious new office, I reflected what a relief it was not to have to worry any more about the actual organization of polo. The RCBPC already had a very good Polo Manager in Michael Amoore, and I made it clear to him from the start that I would be dealing only with sponsorship, not the day-to-day running of polo. My job, in a nutshell, was to exploit sponsorship opportunities and to ensure that, in increasing the profile of the club, everything to do with sponsors and presentations matched the standard of excellence we had achieved at the Guards Polo Club. I was still playing polo, but less frequently which left me time still to deal with the Prince of Wales's polo activities.

The highlight of my time at the RCBPC was the Gulf Trust Polo Day in 1991, in which I had persuaded the Prince of Wales to take part. The Gulf Trust was set up to give support to families who had suffered as a result of the war. The Gulf Trust authorities were excited about the prospect, and wondered, quite naturally, what sort of funds we expected to raise. Proudly, I was able to quote them a forecast of about £400,000. I had already had a verbal agreement from the Kuwaiti government that they would donate £500,000, so I thought we were completely home and dry as far as fund-raising was concerned. The service chiefs agreed to provide military bands, a fly-past of Tornado jets, a helicopter display, parachutists from the Red Devils, a display of tanks around the grounds, practically anything I asked for. It was turning out to be a great day for the services!

It was also a terrific day for the tabloids. On the 7th Armoured Brigade team was a certain Major James Hewitt of the Life Guards. He had recently had some unpleasant and unnecessary publicity in connection with the Princess of Wales. Playing against him, on the 4th Armoured Brigade team, was the Prince of Wales. 'Don't let James take part,' certain people advised me. 'It could be disastrous.' I took no notice. Major Hewitt was a good polo player, a friend of mine who had commanded his squadron brilliantly in the Gulf war. I saw no reason why he shouldn't play. I did, however, take the precaution of mentioning it to the Prince of Wales one day on the polo ground. 'Did you know James Hewitt will be playing against your team, sir?' I remarked casually. The Prince of Wales just shrugged his shoulders as if to say, 'So what?'

One month before the big day, I hit a huge snag. Despite endless telephone calls and faxes, the promised donation of £500,000 from the Kuwaiti government had failed to materialize, and I was kicking myself for not insisting that the original agreement had been confirmed in writing. I had to go back, almost cap in hand, to the various service chiefs and tell them we were unlikely to receive even a fraction of the money we had hoped for.

'We'll be lucky to get £20,000,' I said. 'And that will have to come from the sales of tables for luncheon.' I took the problem to my number one contact, Field Marshal Sir John Chappell. 'Do you want me to cancel?' I asked.

'No, to hell with the Kuwaitis,' he replied. 'Let's have a show of force. Just get cracking.'

The day itself went without a hitch. The heavens opened, but luckily it was while the 450 people were sitting in the huge marquee having lunch. The sun came out an hour before the match, so play wasn't threatened. The press photographers thought they were in seventh heaven when they managed to get a shot of James Hewitt riding off the Prince of Wales in what they considered a very physical fashion. It was nothing more than a good hard ride-off, which you would expect in a needle match of this sort, but the press didn't know that.

The other highlight of my time at the Royal County of Berkshire Polo Club was the Ladies' International Tournament, held in August 1991, an event which unfortunately acquired more than a whiff of notoriety. When the tournament was suggested, the rest of the staff were dubious about whether it would work. I was never sure if this was because they didn't altogether believe in Lesley Player, who was to organize the event, or whether they thought the idea of bringing together teams of women players from all over the world was impossible.

The dirt hit the fan a year later when the *Sunday Times* Insight team ran a story alleging irregularities over the receipt of funds. There was absolutely no truth in these allegations, as the Charity Commissioners later reported, but the damage was done. At the same time, some unsavoury stories concerning myself and Miss Player appeared in the press. Our sponsors, believing that if you throw enough dirt some of it will stick, decided to withdraw their support.

Bryan Morrison rightly took the view that as far as the funds were concerned, there was no case to answer. He explored the possibility of the RCBPC running the Ladies' Tournament themselves, on a slightly different basis. In the end, they decided it was not worthwhile. Bryan was sensitive about adverse publicity and I know I made mistakes. I was criticized by the Establishment for getting sponsors into the RCBPC only because I was able to promise them attendances by Sarah or the Prince of Wales. I was accused of prostituting members of the Royal Family. This was nonsense. Those members of the Royal Family knew what was going on. They had already pledged to support the charities. It's a fact of life that the presence of a member of the Royal Family at a charity event will draw a larger crowd and raise a great deal more money.

Alas, my days at the RCBPC came to an end in March 1993. Due to the recession, few sponsors were available for the coming season. Bryan Morrison called me into a meeting at which we agreed that he could no longer justify my salary as Director of Sponsorship. Contrary to what everyone thought at the time, my reasons for leaving had absolutely nothing to do with the publication of a book by Lesley Player, detailing an alleged affair with me, or because I had stopped being Polo Manager to the Prince of Wales. The reasons were purely economic.

Polo has given me some low moments, but also some of the best and most exciting times of my life. It has taken me all over the world. I have played polo in sixteen countries including some unlikely venues such as Zambia, Cyprus and Finland – I even managed to play when in Aden, on packed sand near the airfield at Khormaskar. Lord Cowdray organized and paid for two memorable trips, one to Chicago in 1962, and another to the Argentine to play in a 30-handicap series against the Argentine and America in Buenos Aires in 1966. It was a marvellous experience to go to the Argentine. Susie accompanied me and we were able to get out and visit the countryside. I loved the wildness and freedom of the landscape, and the warmth of the people. Little was I to know then that this was the country where Susie would one day take up permanent residence.

Another occasion I remember vividly was when I was playing in India with my friend V.P. Singh, who commanded the President's Bodyguard, at the Jaipur polo ground in New Delhi. The ground is situated right next to a golf course – no ordinary course but a highly exclusive one, lovingly maintained, reserved for the use of senior officers in the Indian services only. Generals, admirals and air marshals could be spotted daily, accompanied by their Indian caddies lugging hundreds of pounds' worth of expensive equipment around the course. One of the greens was only about sixty yards behind the goal posts on the polo field, and I was fascinated to observe the various rituals of golf going on before our match began.

For one of the chukkas I was given a pony that I had been told was quite strong. I soon realized what they meant. I was galloping flat out towards the goal that backed onto the golf course, when disaster struck. One of the reins snapped. I had no brakes, only one method of steering and only one rein. The horse thought it was all marvellous. With no pressure on its mouth, it must have thought it was Pegasus. On and on it flew, beyond the goal line, straight towards the golf course. Ahead, on the immaculately tended green, were four senior officers, plus caddies, all lining up to sink their putts.

'Look out!' I shouted, as I careered towards them on this crazy horse, totally out of control. As we tore through the lot of them, these formal senior officers, complete with panic-stricken caddies, ran for dear life scattering clubs and balls in all directions. After a few frantic circuits of the golf course, my horse decided to gallop straight back to its friends in the pony lines, where it promptly stopped. There was an enormous cheer from the Indian grooms, who thought the spectacle of an English major dispersing the service chiefs off the green was the funniest thing they had ever witnessed, and from V.P. Singh who had become a little concerned as to whether he would ever see me again. None of them realized that a rein had broken – they all thought the horse had gone completely mad! I played this particular horse again and he was a very good pony, a pleasure to ride, and, indeed, quite strong. Needless to say, before I mounted him on this subsequent occasion, I made a very thorough check of his reins.

It was V.P. Singh who introduced me to a day of sport that was to be one of the most exhilarating of my entire life – and one that was never to be repeated. On a polo visit to India, in the late sixties, V.P. greeted me with some exciting news. 'In about a week's time,' he announced, 'we're going pig sticking.' I'd read stories about the cavalry in India participating in this most unusual sport, and I'd heard about the renowned Kadir Cup, awarded to the champion of pig sticking. I couldn't wait to give it a try; from accounts I had read, it sounded like a fast and dangerous cross between polo and hunting. We set off the day before; the plan was to camp overnight on the banks of the Ganges in preparation for an early start the following day. There were twelve of us altogether – myself, V.P., a friend of his, plus eight young NCOs from the President's Bodyguard and their instructor. We rode for several hours, arriving in due course at a tented camp with several bearers in attendance. The tents were large and comfortable.

V.P. said, 'Now, this is the plan. We'll have a drink, then dinner, and we'll go to bed quite early because at 3.30 a.m. we're getting up. Then the first thing we'll do is swim the Ganges.'

At the appointed ungodly hour, in the pitch dark, we were woken by one of the bearers with a cup of strong Indian tea. It was still cold and we dressed at V.P.'s suggestion in boots, breeches and a jersey. All of us, including the NCOs, wore hard hats; we'd heard of the dangers and weren't taking any chances. As an added encumbrance, we were equipped with long lances.

'Follow me,' said V.P. After about three hundred yards he rode straight off the bank into the murky swollen waters of the Ganges, still in darkness, and began to make for the opposite side, some hundred yards away. I suspected and prayed that the horses had done this before and knew the procedure; once they were out of their depth, you had to slide backwards over the saddle and hold on to their tails as they swam. Once on the other side, you hoped you'd be able to get back on to the soaking horse – which I couldn't – or you'd be able to catch it to remount – which I could. All this time, you were still hanging on to your lance. One or two of the NCOs let their horses go, but horses, being what they are, just follow all the rest.

With our clothes sopping wet and our boots full of water, we felt pretty chilly by now, but we knew that in a couple of hours it would get hotter and hotter. We rode on uncomfortably, stopping at around 7 a.m. for a much-needed breakfast of omelettes and soft drinks, which seemed miraculously to materialize out of various packs carried by the NCOs.

We rode for about four hours before we reached the pig sticking area and by then the sun was up and all of us were drying off fast and stickily, boots still squelching. We had halted at a sparse, scrubby part of the countryside, stretching for miles on either side with few bushes or trees. V.P.'s guide had already recced the area and knew it harboured several wild pigs living in the undergrowth. This came up to the horses' knees, and the rest of the terrain was rough, pitted with potholes, dotted with hillocks and hidden ditches of all sizes, plus overgrown streams for the unwary to plunge into. We formed a long line and began walking our horses over this hazardous countryside.

'Let your horse's head go,' V.P. warned us. 'He's more experienced than you are, and he'll be better able to avoid the holes.'

We proceeded rather like beaters on a pheasant drive. The hope was that sooner or later a pig would get up out of the scrub, at which point the person closest to it would cry, 'Piggo!' That person then became the point of an arrow as we fell in line behind, on either side, for the charge. V.P. had explained that the pig would run straight for about a hundred yards, and then go to the left or right. When this happened the person closest to the pig would become the apex of the arrowhead.

The pigs themselves weren't pink domesticated ones, but huge, hairy, grey and black monsters with wicked-looking incisors and a terrifying demeanour; they weren't too keen on being routed from their dens and needless to say, they ran extremely fast. The horses went fast too: as experienced bodyguard horses, they had seen it all before. So when the first 'Piggo!' went up, I found myself galloping over this treacherous scrub, not knowing where the holes or ditches were, at a phenomenal pace. At first I took no notice of V.P.'s advice, and tried to ride my horse around the holes. After a couple of bad falls – mercifully, without injury – I had learned my lesson. I let the horse do the work and the navigating.

I was relieved that the first pig sighting happened about six men to my left, not in front of me. Throughout this first chase I was part of the pursuing arrowhead and I watched the others carefully to get the idea of what I should be doing. This pig eventually vanished without trace; we stopped to let the steaming horses have a break.

After another soft drink we remounted and set off to a new pig area, an hour's ride away. We had been in the saddle for about six hours, yet we were so exhilarated by that first hunt, that we had completely forgotten the nightmare of the Ganges swim, the sticky breeches, and the knowledge that it would be at least a six-hour ride back to camp.

'Piggo!' The next chase lasted forty minutes, absolutely flat out. At one moment I led the arrow for about two hundred yards, a tremendous experience. We had also come upon a well-disguised stream into which V.P. went headlong. Worried that he might be injured, I pulled up to see the amazing spectacle of my friend and host emerging from the dank water covered from head to toe in green slime.

'What the hell have you stopped for?' he shouted at me. 'Carry on!'

Eventually we cornered a pig which had got itself into some rushes. Surrounding it at a distance of some twenty-five yards we stood with lances up, mindful of V.P.'s earlier instructions to wait. We had been told that the pig would charge, and at that moment the order would be given to lower the lances, otherwise the pig could come up under a horse and slash its belly.

After two or three minutes the pig stirred. This was all too much for some of the NCOs who were eager to impress. At the first quiver of movement, with lances lowered, shouting excitedly, they charged at the pig. One of them stuck it behind the shoulders and killed it.

V.P. decided it was time to get back to camp. We were tired, so were the horses, and practically all of us had fallen off at some stage. We knew the return journey was going to take about eight hours, including swimming the Ganges.

By the time we got back to camp we were completely exhausted. The horses had picked up because they knew they were going home, and the NCOs were in high spirits because they had put up a good show, but I'd absolutely had it. I am sure my description of this day will seem woefully inadequate to anyone who has taken part in proper pig sticking in India, but for me it was the most exhilarating day I've ever spent on a horse.

These days, my attitude towards killing animals has changed totally, and with the benefit of hindsight I'm surprised that I enjoyed the pig-sticking so much. At the time I felt the experience would be one of the highlights of my life. Now my feelings are more mixed.

Playing polo in England has only been made possible by the help and hard work of a loyal support team, in particular George Smith who worked for me for twenty-eight years. George was a trooper in 2 Troop, the Life Guards Mounted Squadron at Knightsbridge Barracks, when I first went to mounted duty. We were each allowed to have a soldier groom, and I needed an assistant to my stud groom Ralph Cole. When Ralph retired, George took over. George is a quiet person whose only interest, apart from his family, is getting on with his polo work. Over the years, I cannot remember any harsh words being uttered between us, although George was the first person to let me know when I had played badly. The horses were always beautifully groomed, with faultless tack. The many girl grooms (including his wife) who worked with George soon adapted to his high standards and learned to love the horses as he did. I am so pleased that after all these years, as I no longer play polo in England, George has an excellent position organizing the up-and-coming Anstey Polo Club in Wiltshire – it's his just reward for putting up with me for so long.

Another vital member of my support team was Colin Missenden. We served together when he was a corporal major and Master Saddler to the Household Cavalry at Knightsbridge Barracks. Colin has been responsible for keeping my tack in superb condition, and after he left the army, it was with great pleasure that I helped get him a position with the Olympic Way at Harrods. Colin took over looking after the Prince of Wales's saddlery, which led to the Harrods saddlery department receiving the Royal Warrant. Colin has also been a tremendous friend and support throughout the years.

Horses cannot play unless their feet are in superb condition, and Bill Nailor has been my farrier for the last eighteen years. Bill still looks after the children's horses on the farm. I cannot forget, either, the tremendous support I've had from the farm staff for as long as there have been polo ponies at Dummer.

It would be fair to say that polo has knocked me about, but I hadn't thought how much until Jean Rook of the *Daily Express* came down to the Guards Polo Club to interview me. As I changed shirts, a photographer took a shot of my torso. The newspaper published the picture and described my polo injuries; they drew arrows pointing to each part of my body until I looked like Saint Sebastian. After thirty-nine years of playing a relatively dangerous game, you expect some injuries, but when I saw this photo I realized just how many there had been. A broken neck, only one tendon in one arm, no cartilages in the knees, half a kneecap, a smashed nose, screwed-in teeth, broken toes and fingers . . . the list goes on.

When I began playing polo in 1954, and wrote to my father

from Egypt asking him to sell my point-to-point horses, the truth was that I was beginning to get rather windy about competing the following season. My parents and various girlfriends must have become so bored having to inspect a groaning Ronald in the back of an ambulance after practically every race meeting. Little did I know that I was to suffer far greater injuries playing polo than I ever did point-to-pointing. I broke my neck in 1972, and have been officially banned from playing polo ever since. As frequently happens, the horse came down and I landed with my head in one position and my body twisted in another. I wasn't aware that I had done anything particularly serious, so I got up and went on playing. I must have played about four more chukkas – forty-five minutes altogether. Towards the end of the game, I knew that something peculiar was going on because I was beginning to lose the use of my left side and having difficulty holding the reins. I couldn't raise my left arm, or grip with my left leg.

I was committed to playing polo in Cheshire the following weekend, and this I did, even though I was feeling terrible and the injuries did not seem to be abating. I did not say anything to my family, in case they stopped me playing. On the Monday after the Cheshire polo match, nine days after the original accident, I came to the reluctant conclusion that my body wasn't making a very good job of mending itself, so I took myself off to Winchester Hospital and let the doctors check me over.

They were horrified. X-rays revealed I had broken a bone in my neck, which had paralysed the whole of my left side. They couldn't believe I had been walking around for a week, let alone that I had played polo. For three months I couldn't move my left arm or leg more than a couple of inches. I went to see three specialists who all said, 'No, sorry, Major Ferguson, but you'll never ride again.' They put me on painkillers and sleeping pills and I became a complete monster, impossible to live with. For someone whose whole life depended upon physical activity, it was a living death sentence and I became severely depressed.

One day, I was told about a New Zealander called Hugh Burry who had a year's tenure in orthopaedics at Guy's Hospital, an ex All Black rugby player who specialized in sporting injuries. I went along to Guy's to see him.

'Well, there's just that chance,' he said. The minute he uttered those words, my life changed. During that first month of treatment I literally cried from a combination of pain and frustration, although more accurately from the latter as I had got used to the pain. Then there was a slow but definite improvement, and gradually I took myself off the painkillers and sleeping pills. Steadily and surely I got better and turned into a human being again. By the following April, I was back on the polo ground, playing with Ronnie Driver in Cannes.

CHAPTER SIX

Major in the Life Guards

THROUGHOUT the early sixties my army career proceeded at a fairly well-ordered pace. From my job as Staff Captain, Household Division on Horse Guards Parade, I knew that my next position, provided I didn't make a mess of things, would be to take command of the Life Guards Mounted Squadron at Knightsbridge as a major. However, in the winter of 1963/4, trouble in Cyprus escalated. Cyprus had already become an independent republic within the British Commonwealth, with Archbishop Makarios as its first president. The British were allowed to retain sovereign rights over two military bases, Episkopi and Dhekelia, and an air base at Akrotiri. This seemed to suit everyone except the Turkish minority, who responded by murdering as many Greek-Cypriots as they could get their hands on. This happened mostly in the mixed villages that existed on the island. In the towns, there were clear boundaries where one community stopped and the other started.

When Archbishop Makarios called for a Commonwealth peace-keeping force, I knew it was likely that our regiment, which was on strategic reserve, would be involved. I was playing polo in India with an army team when I received a telegram in Delhi saying that I had to be available to take over command of A Squadron from Major William Edgedale, whom I had known since schooldays. The date that I was given to fly to Cyprus clashed completely with the polo tour. This looked to be catastrophic for the rest of the team, and for the Indian teams who were geared up to play against us.

The army's priorities were clearly not the same as mine! I managed to persuade them to let me fly out on a later date. This gave me a chance to finish the polo tour, get back to England for a few days' leave and spend some time with Susie and the girls.

My first experiences of the island were less than idyllic. The regiment was in a God-awful place called Goat Shit Camp, a miserable tented affair set in a barren rock-strewn area, as far removed as possible from any holiday brochure idea of Cyprus. We listened, daily and desperately to the BBC World Service for news of United Nations decisions about the political situation. We knew that if it was decided to send a United Nations peace-keeping force, we would be part of it, swapping our Life Guards black berets for the pale blue ones of the United Nations. It would also mean that instead of being out there for a few weeks on emergency peace-keeping duties, our tour would be extended for an indefinite length of time. Even now, every time I hear 'Lillibullero' – the theme tune to the World Service news – I'm transported back to those days of uncertainty and apprehension.

Uppermost in my mind was not just that I had left behind my wife and young daughters, then aged six and four, and there would be no home leave – I was also leaving behind the forthcoming English polo season. I had been invited to play in a great team, consisting of Prince Philip, Patrick Beresford, myself and John Cavanagh, from Argentina. I also had a fine string of carefully schooled ponies, ably looked after at Dummer by Trooper George Smith. All I needed was to be there. Instead, after our sojourn at Goat Shit Camp, A Squadron moved to a semi-permanent camp near Famagusta. This was in the north-east of the island, an area known as the 'Panhandle', unquestionably the prettiest part.

The Secretary General of the United Nations, U Thant, made his decision and we became part of the United Nations peace-keeping force. I was responsible for the mixed town of Famagusta and the Turkish quarter, and for the whole of the Panhandle, which included numerous mixed villages. Much of our time was spent sorting out problems between villages, such as who stole whose sheep or goat. However trivial these problems seemed at the time, they could easily escalate into violence.

Within Famagusta was a walled Turkish compound that was forbidden to the Greeks. The head Turkish representative was a man called Dr Sami. Not surprisingly, I found it difficult to get him together with the Greek Colonel of Police. I spent hours having meetings with one side or the other. One day I decided I was fed up with all this to-ing and fro-ing, so I arranged a beach barbecue and invited each man without telling the other. There was, of course, the chance that one might turn up and drive away when he saw the other, but I thought it a risk worth taking in the interests of diplomacy. I organized proper tables, white tablecloths and the best food we could get our hands on, the whole event stage-managed courtesy of UN funds.

When Dr Sami and the Greek Colonel arrived, they were pretty surprised to see each other. I held my breath. Before they could say anything, I introduced them to each other and to my fellow officers and gave them a drink. I welcomed them with as much British bullshit and good manners as I could muster, with squadron police staff opening car doors, saluting and generally putting on a show. Having kept back a number of men to meet and greet our VIPs I'd then sent out five armoured-car troops on various duties around the area. Once the Greeks and Turks had safely arrived, the troops were given the signal to come roaring into the barbecue area, one armoured-car after the other. In a cloud of dust, aerials and flags flying, they represented a dramatic show of strength and unity. Our guests were suitably impressed.

We had an excellent barbecue with no speeches, as the

object of the whole exercise had been to get these two men to sit down at the same table together. After lunch Dr Sami, the Greek Colonel and I agreed that the next meeting would take place in the Greek Colonel's office, and the following week we would all go into the Turkish area. It led to a much better understanding between the two sides.

When we moved on to Zyyi (pronounced Ziggy), Willie Loyd became my second in command. This was the beginning of a great friendship that has lasted ever since – both in and out of the army and on and off the polo field.

Zyyi was another area where our main duties were to keep the peace between neighbouring and feuding mixed villages. It was a permanent camp with wooden buildings, and we had the extra delight of our own cinema, showing three films a week. Blood-and-thunder movies were the norm – if we made a mistake and showed a film that was on the sentimental side, it would be loudly booed by our highly discriminating and cultured audience.

At Zyyi the weather always seemed beautiful. In order to keep everybody fit, I made the first parade of the day a PT one, the men wearing only running shoes and bathing trunks. First we went for a two-mile run, ending up at the foot of the fishermen's pier. This was half a mile long with a drop of twenty-five feet at the end, straight into deep water. At this point the non-swimmers fell out, but the rest of us took off our running shoes and ran down to the end, jumping straight into the water.

During my time in Cyprus I like to think that I built a good relationship with my men and with the local villagers as well. I was known as Major Tractor: the farmers boasted among their agricultural machinery a number of ancient Ferguson tractors and they assumed we all came from the same source. I seemed to spend hours with the villagers, both Greek and Turkish, drinking cups of thick sweet coffee and accepting their offerings of sweetmeats and sticky buns.

Polo wasn't lost to me – a certain amount was played in Akrotiri, as the entire regimental team of 1963 was on the island. There was one match when I had broken my hand and was not officially allowed to play, so I joined the RAF team instead, having first dosed myself up with pain-killing injections. Much to the army's fury, the RAF won – they had never had anyone of my calibre playing before, and they took full advantage of it. General Peter Young, who was commanding the sovereign troops, was absolutely furious: the army had never been beaten at polo before.

At the end of October, A Squadron was relieved by the 2nd Royal Tank Regiment. When it came to the handover, instead of writing reams of boring reports, I had the idea of presenting a kind of Handover Question Time. I assembled key squadron headquarters personnel, together with Sergeant Dick Tracy, Corporal of Horse Bill Johnson and Corporal Walsh, the squadron's Master Cook. Our team managed to answer all the complicated and technical questions until we were asked where they could find the Zyyi village head man. He was, in fact, ably deployed and working happily in the Officers' Mess kitchen.

After the handover, on Guy Fawkes' Day, we flew from Akrotiri to Lyneham in Wiltshire for a month's leave. Coming back to England in November from Cyprus was like walking into a refrigerator. Susie and I went to see a huge fireworks display that the regiment put on in the Cavalry Parade Ground at Windsor Great Park. It was good to be back. I'd been away from my family for eleven months, and the girls seemed to have grown almost beyond recognition. It must also have been a comfort for my mother to have me back, as my father, who had been ill with leukaemia for some time, had suffered two strokes and was confined to a nursing home in Winchester. I was shocked to see how much he had changed in the months I had been away.

I visited him as much as I could after my return from

Cyprus, taking time off whenever possible. That August, he died. I still miss his wise, guiding presence that did so much to encourage me as a young man. My parents had moved from Dummer House to the smaller Dummer Down Farm some years previously. Upon Father's death, I inherited his farming business, which comprised 876 acres. I had some serious thinking to do about my future.

Upon my return from Cyprus, I had gone back to the training squadron at Combermere Barracks for a year, then returned for my second tour of duty commanding the mounted squadron at Knightsbridge Barracks, then temporarily rehoused in Wellington Barracks, as Knightsbridge was being rebuilt. Many of my friends had already left the army in search of pastures and business ventures new, and I was seriously considering joining them. I'd twice failed part of the exam I needed to be promoted to substantive major. I'd had no problem with the practical side – I had passed with flying colours – but if I wanted eventually to command my regiment, as my father and grandfather had, I needed to get through the written exam. As usual, I had spent my time having fun instead of working. It was a blow to my pride, but it wasn't the end of the world. If I had passed, I would have had to take a staff job, both before and after taking command, and sitting behind a desk isn't my favourite activity.

After my father's death, I also had to deal with the problem of being an absentee landlord for Dummer Down so, in 1968, with mixed feelings, I made arrangements to leave the army. I may not have passed out of Sandhurst with the full military parade, but I certainly made up for it before I left the army. It was pure luck for me that in 1968 the Ministry of Defence was approached by an American organization called Columbia Festivals who had already taken a number of military bands to play on tour in America. They decided they would like to mount an even more spectacular show –

these were the days when anything British was still highly rated – and stage a full military tattoo.

The Ministry of Defence agreed that in principle they could have the mounted band of the Household Cavalry, including Life Guards, Blues and Royals – some seventy-eight horses – plus the pipes and drums of the Highland Fusiliers and a detachment of junior guardsmen from Pirbright. It was decided that I should command this detachment, together with an officer from the Highland Fusiliers, and an officer from the junior guardsmen. It was a huge project: together with other Household Cavalry officers and our own veterinary surgeon, we numbered 120 men.

In September we flew Air France to Philadelphia in three aeroplanes – two for the horses, one for ourselves. The Air France representative who helped us make all the arrangements was a wonderful woman called Maria Huck whose name was deliberately mispronounced by the men. The plan was to spend one week in Philadelphia, two weeks in Madison Square Garden, New York, and one week in Boston Gardens, Boston. It was my first major piece of organization and I was apprehensive.

The show was a cavalcade of pageantry. I helped choose the music in consultation with my friend Major Walter 'Jacko' Jackson, Director of Music. I wanted the show to be bold and different, and chose a selection from *The Jungle Book* much to the surprise of some. It worked perfectly; people were amazed when they saw how we had combined all the elements of the show.

The highlight of the tattoo was the finale, which I'd choreographed myself. We divided into four circles within circles, each circle moving counterclockwise to the one adjacent to it, to appropriately dramatic music. I was positioned in the centre of all of them, in full dress uniform, mounted on my horse, Dolly, with my trumpeter behind. The junior guardsmen marched out of the arena one way and the Highland Fusiliers marched out the other, leaving the Household Cavalry lined up behind me as I saluted the VIPs. I then moved forward, followed by the Household Cavalry who had lined up in pairs – one Life Guard and one Blue. To the tune of 'Land of Hope and Glory', we proceeded slowly down the middle of the arena, and out. At some of the Madison Square Garden performances you could see the audience getting their handkerchiefs out, the whole effect was so dramatic.

At that first paid-for performance, however, we hit a snag. What none of us had thought of was what we should do for an encore. That first night, as soon as the men and horses had gone out, there were cries of 'More! Encore!' We had to think quickly. We couldn't possibly reassemble the men and horses who had already galloped out. There was only one thing to do.

'Jacko,' I said, 'I'm going to go back into the arena alone, salute and then gallop out. Can you come up with some appropriate music?'

Jacko rushed back and hummed to the band the tune he had chosen to accompany my moment of glory. I rode back in, to great cheers and yells, and saluted the VIPs and the audience on all sides. Then, brandishing my sword, I galloped out at full speed with the band playing the music that Jacko had selected – the *Lone Ranger* theme. This improvised encore happened every night for the following thirty-five performances, and each time we had a standing ovation.

One night in New York, Mayor John Lindsay took the salute. After the performance I invited him to have a look around the stables backstage.

'I invite you to parade through my city,' he said. I agreed readily.

The chosen day dawned beautifully bright and sunny and when the horses got to the bottom of the spiral ramp you could see them prick up their ears and blink as they emerged into the first real daylight they had seen for ten days. It had been decided that we would parade up 6th Avenue and down 7th. After lengthy discussions with the Chief of Police, both avenues were closed. The disruption this caused was immense; the whole city came to a grinding halt. It was quite a moment, riding in front of the men with both bands marching behind, as we progressed slowly along those two great avenues to the cheers of the crowds.

From New York, it was off to Boston Gardens for our final round of performances. All this time I was aware that, like the sand in an hourglass, my time in the army was fast running out. I had already extended my departure by a month to encompass the tattoo. I would be returning to quit what had been my life for twenty years.

There were two encores on our last night. The commentator had already announced that not only was it the last parade for the Tattoo, it would be the last parade for its Director as well. The event was highly charged. After it was over and the audience had left, with the men occupied in looking after the horses or getting changed, I took a few moments to wander around the arena by myself. I realized then how much I had been living on my nerves. Letting all the tension go at last, the tears welled up and streamed down my face. I couldn't do it anywhere else, in case any of the men saw. Perhaps they did, but no one said a word.

CHAPTER SEVEN

Royally Entertained

IN THE SIXTIES, when I was regularly playing polo with Prince Philip's team and living at nearby Lowood, we were honoured to be able to invite the Queen to dinner at our house on one or two occasions. It is quite normal for Her Majesty to attend private dinner parties at friends' houses, and she enjoys it immensely. We would usually invite about eight other people to Lowood, friends we had in common with the Queen or people we thought she would enjoy meeting.

A telephone call to Windsor Castle would establish what the Queen would be wearing – if it was a short evening dress, Susie and the other female guests would adopt the same style. The men would all be in black tie. When planning the menu, we would choose food we knew the Queen liked, having been entertained ourselves at Sandringham or Windsor. At home the Queen chooses her own menus, so we knew she favours fairly plain food (though not quite plain enough for my taste.) We tended to avoid serving game, because she would have had so much of it. The meal was prepared at Lowood by our cook, or we would employ someone to cook the dinner. The table would be laid with our usual silver and crystal – my theory is that what's been good enough for us is good enough for anybody else. We wouldn't have dreamed of hiring that for the occasion.

It is common etiquette for the other guests to arrive before the Queen, but she wouldn't mind if someone was late; she is a very understanding woman. The Queen's private secretary would have informed us at what time she planned to arrive. Susie would then ask our other guests to arrive half an hour earlier. During the introductions, the only difference between this and other dinner parties would be that the guests would bow or curtsy. After about twenty minutes of chat we would go into dinner. As host, I would be sitting next to the Queen. As we never employed a butler or footmen, at an ordinary dinner party I would be getting up every two seconds to fill people's glasses. With Her Majesty as a guest I would avoid that by having staff to wait at the table; you don't exactly entertain the Queen every day of your life.

Neither Susie nor I were drinkers, so we didn't have a proper cellar. I would ring up the chief steward at Windsor Castle and ask him what the Queen liked – as simple as that. There would be a starter, a main course and a pudding. The Queen doesn't eat puddings, so she would have cheese instead. In country houses then, the women used to 'withdraw' after dinner, leaving the men to drink their port and talk mostly rubbish. That sort of thing bores the Queen, so I used to hurry it along. Prince Philip didn't enjoy it any more than did I. I've now banned the custom in our household.

During coffee, if people hadn't talked to the Queen before or during dinner, Susie or I would move them next to her. One topic that might be discussed was race horses. The Queen is extremely knowledgeable about everything to do with bloodstock. My mother, who knew several of her ladies-in-waiting, tells an extremely funny anecdote concerning a royal visit to one of the Newmarket studs. The Queen, as usual, took an intense interest in everything, inspecting the horses, the stables, the tack. Then she noticed something hanging on a wall.

'What is that?' she asked.

Members of the stud staff shifted in an agony of embarrassment. Her Majesty had just pointed to an important piece of stud equipment, an artificial mare's vagina. Eventually one of them plucked up courage and explained it to the Queen. To their relief, she roared with laughter.

'Oh, well.' She shrugged. 'Ask a silly question . . .'

During the sixties at Lowood, we always gave a dance during Ascot week for our guests. One year the Queen brought her own house party to join us. Instead of a formal dinner, we had a buffet supper. For dancing, we constructed an awning, tacked onto the children's playroom, extending out to the garden to form the 'ballroom', we had a three-piece band to play, a bar out in the garden – and we prayed for fine weather.

When the Queen arrived, as her host, I first invited her to dance. Prince Philip went off to do his own thing – usually he would make a beeline for the prettiest girl on the dance floor. He certainly found my wife Susie's company much more enticing than mine. I would keep an eye on the Queen to make sure she was enjoying herself. She was there with our friends and those friends of hers who were making up her house party, so it was all very relaxed. Little did I know then that my daughter Sarah, fast asleep upstairs in the nursery, would one day herself be invited to join the Queen's Ascot house party and begin a romance that was to change all our lives irrevocably.

The Queen may be grand, but not in other people's homes, and certainly not in her own home. If one of her dogs makes a mess, for example, instead of sending for someone to clean it up, the Queen will go off and get the water and cloths and do it herself. She is a capable, practical, and an extremely kind person. She showed great understanding and sympathy one year when Susie and I were invited to Sandringham to shoot, two days after I arrived back from a polo tour in India. As it turned out, the aeroplane broke down in Bahrain and we were delayed for forty-eight hours. When I landed at Heathrow I was met by Susie, and we had to drive straight to Norfolk.

The weekend was a nightmare. It was January, very cold, and I had come straight from the extreme heat of India. Sandringham is a warm house, so I spent the whole time outside being cold and tired or inside being hot and tired. I felt permanently exhausted. The food at Sandringham is rich as far as I'm concerned; I can't stand Indian food, so in India I'd been living entirely on simple things like egg and chips. Now the combination of food, exhaustion and central heating meant I was dropping off to sleep at every available opportunity. On the first day's shooting, I was so tired and disorientated, I nodded off while sitting on a shooting stick just before a drive. The Queen noticed the problems I was having. She was very sympathetic and allowed me to retreat after tea to have a rest before dinner. Normally, if you are a guest at a royal house party, you can't just nip off and have a sleep whenever you feel like it. If I hadn't been able to do this, I don't know how I would have survived.

There would usually be about eight other guests at Sandringham. After dinner, for which we always changed, we sometimes had a film screening. Sandringham has its own built-in cinema seating about forty people. Films chosen were always the latest, often well ahead of their general release date, and the Queen invited her staff to come in and watch as well.

Weekends at Sandringham meant a lot of eating: a proper country-house breakfast with kippers, eggs, bacon, all the trimmings, served from silver salvers topped with domed lids; lunches in a shooting lodge or hut on the estate; then, when shooting was over, a traditional tea, with sandwiches and cakes, and a few hours later, dinner. Spending a weekend with the Queen also meant putting on and taking off a lot of different outfits.

I have only been to Balmoral once to discuss a forthcoming polo season with the Prince of Wales when he was shooting grouse up in the hills. Balmoral is a lovely turreted castle, approached through wrought-iron gates up a long drive lined with rhododendron bushes and pine trees. There is a huge expanse of lawn in front of the house, and a tranquil backdrop of blue- and purple-tinged hills covered with heather behind it. The surroundings are peaceful and beautiful, with gurgling streams full of leaping salmon.

I didn't shoot with Prince Charles that day but sat with the toddler, Prince William, in the butts. I had given up shooting more than twenty years before. Not long after we moved to Dummer, I had taken part in a particularly murderous low-flying pheasant shoot. In the middle of the day, I decided to stop. At the time, I was fairly committed, with a gun in one syndicate, half a gun in another, and my own at Dummer. But my lovely black labrador, Tweed, the only gun dog I ever owned, had just died of jaundice, and, with his death, my heart had gone out of the sport. Half the fun of shooting was to have your dog with you, picking up afterwards. When I got home that day, I went straight to my study and rang up all the people who had invited me to shoot in the future. While all this was going on, Susie kept coming into the study and asking me what I was doing.

'I'll tell you afterwards, when I've finished,' I said.

I managed to sell my gun for the rest of the season, and the half gun too. I spent two hours on the telephone. At the back of my mind, I was all too aware of an invitation to shoot at Sandringham three weeks hence. Not wanting to seem hypocritical, my last telephone call was to Prince Philip.

'I'm very sorry, sir,' I said, 'I'm giving up shooting, so I will have to turn down your invitation.'

I went out and told Susie what I had done.

'What are you talking about?' she said, amazed.

'I've given up shooting,' I said. 'I've sold my gun in the syndicate and turned down all the invitations.'

There was a pause. 'Even Sandringham?' she asked finally. 'How could you?' For forty-eight hours, Susie refused to speak to me. If I was to give up shooting, she reasoned, I could at least have waited until after the Sandringham weekend!

I gave up because I had suddenly decided that I no longer had the right to take an animal's or bird's life. Now I don't even kill flies, although I do encourage my dogs to chase and kill rats because they're a hazard to the farm and to health. I can hardly believe I once went pig sticking, though as I've admitted earlier, I loved it at the time.

About two days after I had decided to give up, some friends were coming to shoot at Dummer. I had to honour that commitment, so I turned myself into head beater for the day. This was good experience: I hadn't before realized what a difficult job it is to do properly. Nothing gave me more pleasure than sending birds right over the heads of friends who stood little chance of hitting them. When it came to the expert shots, I sent the birds in the opposite direction.

CHAPTER EIGHT

Father and Son – Polo Memories of the Duke of Edinburgh and the Prince of Wales

I FIRST MET Prince Philip when I was invited to join his polo team; our relationship was strictly a sporting one, but because of it, Susie and I were invited to shoot at Sandringham a few times during the sixties, and one summer we were also invited to join the Queen's house party at Royal Ascot. I always suspected that Prince Philip had an eye for Susie. Certainly, they remain friends to this day.

My earliest impression of the Duke of Edinburgh was of a man who lacked patience. I reported earlier his altercation with my father umpiring at polo after the war.

As a father myself, I have noticed the lack of closeness between the royal princes and Prince Philip. Whereas the Queen is a sympathetic person, I don't feel that Prince Philip is the sort of parent to whom the children would pour out their problems. They seem wary of him. Certainly I was aware of potential difficulties arising over simple things and before I asked him anything, I knew it would be wise to have all the facts at my fingertips concerning the subject under discussion.

His manner is pretty abrupt, but it seems to lack the humanity and humour that I hope lies beneath my rather

The poser

Engagement photo at Dummer House.

Guard of honour.

The bride with her father, arriving at St. Margaret's, Westminster.

The honeymoon, Kitzbühel.

Top: Lowood, our first home.

Above: Aden, where I was posted in 1958

Right: The tanker on which Susie and I returned to Aden, somewhat uncomfortably, after my knee operation.

Exposing myself to the rays.

Palm trees and sunshine. 'A soldier's
life is terrible hard, says Alice.'

Glowing with happiness and health.

Pig-sticking in India, with my friend and host VP (now Brigadier Singh).

Cyprus, Zyyi camp.

With Willie Loyd. We were known as Pinky and Perky (I was Perky).

Top: British Army versus Jaipur, in Jaipur.

Left: With the late Trevor Howard, advising on the film *The Charge of the Light Brigade.*

Below, left: Wellington Barracks, playing the fool.

Below, right: Before an all-ranks party. I seemed to have a permanent tan in those days.

Above, left: Wellington Barracks, with S C M John Cawthorne.

Above, right: State visit by President Tubman of Liberia and Mrs Tubman.

Right: Prince Philip being gallant to my wife.

Below: Windsor Park, with John Cavanagh, Prince Philip and Patrick Beresford.

With Patrick Beresford at an Hawaiian party, Oakbrook, Chicago.

Spectating after playing polo in South Africa.

My favourite photograph of my father, in Scotland with his beloved Tessa.

gruff exterior. If he does make jokes, they appear to be at other people's expense. It is very difficult to know if a member of the Royal Family has said something genuinely funny or not. Surrounded as they are by sycophants, a remark containing the merest touch of humour has the toadies rolling about with glee.

When he makes a statement that he believes is funny, and everyone around him laughs, he is sometimes genuinely shocked by the criticism that follows.

The first time I met the Prince of Wales was at a polo match. I ran into him at Smith's Lawn many times when he came to watch his father play. When Prince Charles started to play polo seriously in 1970, it was obvious he needed someone to co-ordinate his playing. I suppose my background made me the obvious candidate, and gradually I found myself taking on the job. In the end I must have appointed myself as his Polo Manager, an honorary position, and I was proud to be able to serve him in this way for twenty-one years. He is a good player. His highest handicap was four; his father's was five. But then, as in many other things, Prince Philip was a harder, tougher customer than his son.

It is important to understand how much the game means to the Prince of Wales. He doesn't dabble at it; he really works at it, and he could have been a much better player if he had been able to give more time to practise. You need to practise five or six days a week, including the days of play, to keep ahead of the game. The Prince of Wales is a fine horseman, he is strong and he's got guts. He is dedicated to polo; he'll be devastated when he has to give it up for good. I was sorry to hear last January that he had decided to give up competitive polo. My private view is that if he plays only occasionally, as has been announced, it will be even worse for his back, since he won't be polo fit.

As heir to the throne he is a man who lives most of his life in a state of high frustration. Polo was his outlet, his way of letting off steam. He skis, hunts and fishes, but there is nothing in his life that works like polo for getting rid of aggression and tension. It is a team sport, and he liked it because there is no deference, people don't treat him differently. It is also fantastic exercise for someone who has to spend hours at official functions or behind a desk. Like all of us, he likes to win, and he has had to learn to be a good loser. This isn't something that comes naturally to a member of the Royal Family. Incidents of bad sportsmanship that were widely reported in the press, such as the Prince hurling sticks or hats to the ground, or blaming his horse, were always to do with frustration and anger, mostly directed at himself.

As Polo Manager to the Prince of Wales, people would often ask me, 'What do you actually do?'

And in a frivolous way, I'd reply, 'I get him to the right place at the right time, with the right horses, and wearing the right shirt.'

The biggest challenge was putting together his forthcoming schedule of matches. This had to be produced by 1 October the previous year, with days, times and places carefully worked out so they could be absorbed into his programme. The fixtures had to dovetail around his duties and I would find that a fifteen-minute difference in the start time of a match could be crucial. I had to work closely with his staff and although we would make a lot of changes – because of his enormous burden of commitments – in the end, it always worked out.

Polo teams would approach me all the time asking for the Prince of Wales to play, because it obviously added prestige to their team if he did. The number one ground at Windsor was his favourite location, followed by the Ivy Lodge at Cirencester and the Lawns ground at Cowdray.

I was responsible for his ponies, his sticks – even his moods. There were occasions when he arrived at the ground and you could almost see smoke coming out of the top of his head, he was so uptight. If he was low and tired, I had to boost him up, either by making a comment or getting him angry. On other occasions he was buoyant and I'd need to subdue him slightly to make him concentrate. I don't think the Prince of Wales realized when I was trying to manipulate his moods. I would do it by giving him the wrong stick, for example. 'Why on earth can't you give me the right stick,' he'd yell. That was exactly the sort of angry reaction I wanted, to get the adrenalin flowing.

I was a useful whipping boy. The Prince couldn't shout and scream at just anyone, but he could and did take it out on me. When this happened, I would just wander away for a few moments, take a walk round the horse box, and inevitably when I came back he was full of apologies. It took me a short time to get used to him, but I would say that our polo-playing relationship was close. It wasn't so much that he talked to me about polo, it was more that he had a nanny around to look after him; I knew him, knew his moods and knew what he wanted even before he did.

Foreign royal polo tours were great fun. Twice I had the honour of accompanying the Prince of Wales to Australia, several times to America, and also to Brunei for the independence celebrations. In advance of the match, I would need to ride all the horses they were offering to find suitable ones on which he could play. All he had to do was turn up.

I got more than I bargained for on one Australian tour. There were always many kind and generous owners keen to lend their horses to the Prince of Wales, and nowhere was this demonstrated more aptly than one morning when I arrived at the Adelaide Polo Club to select six horses for that afternoon's match. It was February, and the temperature was climbing steadily towards ninety degrees, even at nine in the morning. 'There are the horses,' said the organizers, pointing towards a large corral. I was simply appalled. There must have been sixty all penned in together.

'All of them?' I asked, bearing in mind that as it was February, and I wasn't playing polo on this tour, I was fairly unfit.

'All of them.' They beamed.

That morning I rode sixty horses in three hours, and by the time I finished, I was in an extreme state of exhaustion. I don't know whether it was the Australian sense of humour, or the way things turned out, but it seemed to me that the organizers held back the best horses until the end; of the last ten I rode, I chose six. When I told the Prince of Wales how I'd spent my morning, he laughed. 'It will do you good,' he said.

One memorable foreign tour almost altered the course of history. The Prince of Wales had flown directly to a tournament in Palm Beach, Florida, from a series of gruelling public engagements in Canada. For him, the sudden change of climate would have been particularly acute.

'Get plenty of liquids into you before you play,' I warned him. 'Don't sit in the sun too long.'

He ignored me and spent two hours before the game sitting outside, basking in the warmth of the Florida spring sunshine, having already ridden eight horses in the morning. The afternoon was very hot, about 85°F, with high humidity. It was a hard match, and he refused to take any of the drinks I had organized for him. Towards the end of the match, it was obvious that the Prince was in a bad state. Red in the face, and getting weaker by the chukka, he was just able to attend the presentation of the prizes, but he had to lean on a stick while on the podium. I was concerned; it was obvious that he was suffering from dehydration.

I had seen many instances of this during my tours of duty in the Middle East and Cyprus, so I knew the symptoms. Without further ado, we whisked him back to the house where we were staying.

'He's in a bad way,' announced Paul Officer, his personal

protection officer, having checked the Prince's room. 'He seems to be in a coma.'

We had to move fast. There was no time to call for an ambulance, and we didn't want to draw too much attention to the situation anyway. The only suitable vehicle we had was a blue baggage truck. 'Put him in there,' someone suggested. 'He'll be quite inconspicuous.'

So, wrapped in a duvet and bundled in a truck driven by a sergeant in the Florida State Police, the heir to the throne was driven off to a Palm Beach hospital in what was probably the most undignified journey of his entire life. During that forty-minute journey we went up on pavements, drove through shopping malls, jumped every red light. Half-way through we were met by State Troopers to assist our journey. I was driving a hired car immediately behind the baggage truck with Oliver Everett, the Prince's assistant private secretary. After half a mile or so, I asked Oliver why he was frantically making notes on the back of an envelope.

Barely suppressing the panic in his voice, and making one of the biggest understatements of all time, Oliver explained, 'As his equerry . . . if anything happens to him . . . I would have to make a few telephone calls . . .'

Half-way into the journey, Paul Officer stuck his head out of the baggage truck and gave us the thumbs-up sign, which we rightly interpreted as the Prince having regained consciousness. He was still in a bad state when we reached the hospital, where he was admitted as John Doe. They had already been alerted so there was little procedure to be got through when we arrived. (On every occasion when he played, arrangements had already been made with the nearest hospital. A code word would be chosen and put into operation if necessary.) He was put on a drip, and within minutes he was showing strong signs of recovery. It was a close shave, however, and entirely his fault. In future he took more heed of my advice.

My relationship with Prince Charles, summer and winter, revolved only around his polo activities. I wasn't involved in any other aspect of his life. Of course, I knew a lot about what was going on. Sometimes he would let slip the odd remark. My attitude was that I was there to look after his polo, and I didn't want to be compromised. All of us who worked with him and served him knew about the difficulties, his personal problems, his relationship with Camilla Parker Bowles, though we didn't know the details. But Prince Charles and I never had any personal conversations, either about my life or his.

I got on well with him, even better in the later years, after Sarah married Andrew, because I felt able to be that much tougher with him, about polo, at a time when he needed it. There were so many people around him saying, 'Yes sir, no, sir.' I am not a three-bags-full man. I might have annoyed him once or twice, by being so direct, but I think he appreciated it. I'd never been able to give Prince Philip a bollocking on the polo ground, but Prince Charles was a different matter. I'd say, 'For God's sake, come on now, get stuck in, stop pussyfooting around.'

I had to protect him from people coming up to him at the beginning of a game, and I'd get quite tough about it. He would say, 'Sorry, I've got to go. Nanny tells me I've got to get on with the game,' or, 'Oh God, he's bullying me again,' referring to me. I felt conscious that everyone was spending a great deal of money on his behalf, and you don't get stuck into a game by having social conversations when you arrive late. You have to psych yourself up to play.

All of this I saw as a personal favour to a friend, which made me doubly bitter when it all ended. In February 1993, my position as unpaid, honorary Polo Manager to the Prince of Wales was abruptly terminated in a letter to me from his private secretary. There had been a lot of bad publicity, to put it mildly, concerning a woman called

Lesley Player. Her book had been serialized in a Sunday tabloid, and not long afterwards I heard on the grapevine, from a third party, that the Prince of Wales had decided to dispense with my services.

After serving him faithfully and unquestioningly for twenty-one years, I was appalled by the way it was handled. The Prince of Wales did not have the guts to send for me and tell me straight to my face. Apparently there had been a slip-up – my informant thought I had already received a letter. A couple of days later, it arrived, signed not by the Prince of Wales but by his private secretary. I was sad and disappointed that it then took the Prince five days to pick up the telephone and talk to me. 'Ronald, I just didn't know what to do,' he said. 'I thought it would be for the best.'

'Best for whom?' I asked.

He had let himself down badly in my eyes, and destroyed a lot of the respect I had for him. He wasn't tough enough or strong enough to tackle me directly. The impression I got was that he had been advised to perform a royal version of ethnic cleansing by getting rid of the Ferguson family from his circle. The Establishment was trying to make a new image for him following his separation from the Princess of Wales. The excuse given was that the Prince of Wales was not going to play high goal polo, so there was no longer any requirement for a polo manager. Yet Robert French Blake performed exactly my duties throughout the 1993 polo season.

Prince Charles admitted afterwards that one reason why he had not asked to see me personally was because he was afraid I'd try to persuade him to keep me on. As it happens, I probably wouldn't have. He had failed to take into account – and probably doesn't even know – the amount of time and money that was spent on his organization, the hours I had spent on the ground when he was playing, or the miles I had driven, at my own expense, to get there.

The Prince of Wales is not as stuffy as a lot of people make out, but he's not exactly the life and soul of the party, either. He has lived in an ivory tower, surrounded by toadies, for all these years, and has created jobs for himself because he's got to do something. I don't see him succeeding to the throne, ever. An intensive PR campaign is afoot to try to change his image in the eyes of the media but it isn't working: for the Prince to be portrayed smiling and allowing photographs of him painting, talking to children – it's just not him. The seasoned royal reporters can see right through it. They would much prefer him to be grumpy and stuffy. His toadies ought to be changing their ways by giving the press more information, making him more accessible, rather than trying to change his image.

Certainly the Royal Family have a difficult time ahead of them. I know, for instance, that Prince Charles will never make any major change in his life, such as a divorce, while the Queen Mother is alive. He would never want to do anything to upset his grandmother to whom he is devoted.

CHAPTER NINE

Life Outside the Army, and the End of My Marriage

IN THE AUTUMN of 1968, a week after returning from America, I handed over my squadron to Timothy Gooch, said goodbye to the boys and left the army. The worst of it, after nineteen years, was that my days now had no shape to them, and I badly missed the camaraderie of my men.

That year, the decision had already been taken to move from Lowood to Dummer Down Farm, after my father's death. It was sad to leave the house where the children had spent so many happy times, but I had always regarded Dummer as home; it was where I was brought up. It was great to be in the country again, and Susie was delighted at the prospect of being able to keep her horses there. My mother moved to a cottage in the village and couldn't have been happier, knowing that Dummer Down House would be loved and looked after properly.

My father had sold the first house he owned in the village, Dummer House, in 1958, when he became ill with leukaemia, and the 1,250 acres that went with the property had become too much for him. Dummer Down House was already part of the estate, but at the other end of the village. It was originally a small Queen Anne farmhouse, built in 1817. Susie and I had an extension built onto it when we first moved in, to give us a decent-sized dining room and an extra bedroom.

A question mark hung over exactly what I was going to do with my time. The farm was then a mixed one of about 850 acres, and in the two years that I had been an absent landlord, the farm and the dairy herd had been ably run by Geoffrey Probyn, the farm manager. Geoffrey had taken total control from the time my father first became an invalid, and had continued to his death and since, so he certainly didn't need me wandering about interfering.

There was a winter polo tour to keep me occupied. Horses soon became a large feature of our lives. Apart from Sarah's little Shetland, Nigger (one could never get away with such a name now!), no horses had been kept at Lowood. Now that we were at Dummer, with stables and a proper yard, the flood gates opened. Apart from my polo ponies, about eight of them under the beady eye of groom George Smith, there were ponies for Jane and Sarah. Susie herself became a horse kleptomaniac – she even had horses sent from the Argentine to make into show jumpers. My polo stable was kept separately from everyone else's, but it was horse chaos here. Not unnaturally, this led to some gentle disputes between farm staff and stables.

'If you want to be well looked after round here,' they would cry, 'be a horse.'

Sarah and Jane became accomplished riders and entered all the gymkhanas and other local events. They and their mother hunted regularly, particularly in Warwickshire where we had friends and the hunting was excellent. Sarah's bedroom was filled with rosettes from the competitions she had entered, and at one time she even considered taking up showing and eventing professionally, although the dressage part of eventing bored her. What she loved was the more daredevil side of it all, the cross country and the jumping. We were so proud of her when she competed in the Hickstead All England Schools' Championships on her horse, Spider.

There were tennis and swimming parties for the girls, ski holidays – an idyllic childhood. Christmases at Dummer during those years were always wonderful family occasions, with both the girls' grandmothers present. Jane and Sarah would each be given one of my shooting socks to hang up as a stocking the night before – there was always a huge argument as to whose was the fullest. I liked to arrange a surprise visit to a show or a pantomime – something I still do with my second family. I never let on where we're going until we get there. To their frustration and amusement, I lead them on a circuitous route, sometimes walking straight past the theatre.

'It's here, Dads,' they would cry.

'No it's not,' I'd pretend.

All those horses' mouths to feed cost a fortune, and in 1969 when I was offered a job as a consultant by Nigel Neilson, boss of the public relations firm, Neilson McCarthy, I gladly accepted, to help keep the grain flowing. Nigel thought that I might be useful, having organized the Military Tattoo. My brief was to expand the business, but I don't remember doing anything of the kind. I was good at meeting people but, apart from that, I don't think my contribution was enormous. Even so, I eagerly joined the commuting throng, travelling every day from Basingstoke to 24 Bruton Street, Mayfair. It was something I had always dreaded, but in fact I enjoyed my foray into PR and what I learned there proved useful later on when it came to organizing charity polo matches and sponsorships. Nigel is a very nice man, and I also worked with Beth Barrington Haynes, whom I encountered again when I was at the Guards Polo Club. For the first years of the International Polo Day, which began in 1972, Neilson McCarthy negotiated the contracts, and Beth was directly responsible for working on them.

In 1971, I took up my dream job as Deputy Chairman of the Guards Polo Club. It meant I could be paid for something I really wanted to do.

All did not seem to be going well with my marriage, however. After sixteen years, it had gone through its ups and downs, including a bad time in 1969 when Susie was expecting our longed-for third child. At seven months pregnant, she was diagnosed as having toxaemia and pre-eclampsia. She was rushed into hospital and was there for eight weeks. Tragically, she lost the baby, and very nearly died herself. I was distraught. I booked myself into a room at the hospital and stayed there during the worst times, praying everything would be all right.

Susie was ill for a long time after that, and it was months before she regained any of her former sparkle. Losing this baby seemed to put her into a severe postnatal depression; I was distressed to read later that she blamed me for much of that and accused me of 'womanizing'. Whatever anyone may like to think, I was devoted to my wife and family. I admit there had been the occasional indiscretion, but these amounted to only two brief affairs in sixteen years. Almost any man, married for that length of time, who travelled extensively away from home as I had, would probably admit to the same.

We had both been products of a repressed fifties generation. My mother, with her lynxlike ears, had monitored each creak of every floorboard whenever, as a teenager, I had brought girls home from a party. My army experiences had not been exactly educational as far as the opposite sex was concerned; Susie was only eighteen when we married, so we were two inexperienced young people living through a liberal sixties age of 'free love'. Yet, to say, as Susie has done, that I was a chronic womanizer is not true.

I had known Hector Barrantes as a fine professional polo player for many years and admired him greatly. As a family, we reinforced our friendship when we had stayed at the same hotel as Hector and his wife Luisita at the polo tournament in Deauville in August 1971. It was therefore a terrible shock when we heard the following February that Luisita and their unborn child had been killed in a car crash near Buenos Aires. Hector had badly fractured his leg in the accident, and was near to despair.

Susie and I felt such sadness for him. His tragedy had come not long after our own, and we wanted to help as much as we could, so we invited him to join us on holiday in Corfu that summer. The house party included another Argentinian couple and Jean-Paul Belmondo's daughter Florence, who is one of Sarah's great friends. During that holiday the seeds of a romance between Susie and Hector were sown.

One character trait that Susie shares with both Jane and Sarah is that once they get an idea into their heads, they become obsessed by it. That summer of 1972, Susie decided that she had had enough of me and wanted Hector. I had absolutely no idea of it. As far as I was concerned, Hector was this rather sad man, who had lost his wife, and we as a family had befriended him. We had had a great time in Corfu, but as far as I know, there was nothing going on. It was all in Susie's head.

That September, Susie accompanied me on a polo trip to Scotland; our Dundee relatives were always delighted to see us, and it should have been a happy visit, but I had the feeling that something was wrong. I asked Susie to tell me what was bothering her, and she replied that she thought she was in love with Hector. She wanted to leave me, and be with him.

It was like being dealt a mortal blow. I tried to talk her out of it, tried to get her to see what I thought was sense. I was committed to the polo tour, so I couldn't show my emotions in public, but privately I was in anguish. I loved my family; it wasn't just the prospect of losing Susie, but the thought of splitting everything up – dismantling the wonderful life we had built together – that caused the grief.

Susie had already spoken to my mother about it. Later Mother told me that Susie had said, 'I have to leave now, otherwise the girls will have grown up and gone, and I'll be left all alone with Ronald.'

On our return from Scotland, we lived through some unhappy weeks before Susie finally left Dummer in late 1972 to live in the family house in First Street, Chelsea, taking with her Mrs Cole (wife of Ralph Cole who was then my stud groom) as housekeeper. She took only her clothes and her jewellery. She left the dogs, horses, furniture and most of her personal effects behind. Even then, it was not established that she had gone for good. Jane was fifteen and Sarah thirteen. They were wrapped up in their own world of horses and schoolfriends. None of this would change. They were told that their mother was going off on a temporary basis, and they would see her as much as possible. There was never any question of a custody agreement. Susie didn't want any money, or pay-offs; she didn't want to take any encumbrances into her new life. Jane and Sarah had to accept the new situation, and it must have hurt badly.

Both the girls' grandmothers rallied round – Susie's wonderful mother, Grummy, was never one to let a simple thing like a divorce or a separation get in the way of our relationship, or her involvement with her grandchildren; she provided a lot of support for us all during those first dark days after Susie left.

I even felt sorry for Hector. He was a marked quarry. It had been Susie's idea to leave Dummer, and he had fought tooth and nail to stop her. He didn't want to be the person who broke up our marriage. He even had a meeting with me about it, to try to explain. It was no use, Susie was utterly determined. Hector said to me, 'I don't want to cause anyone unhappiness.' By then, he had little option.

I had always thought of Susie as a loyal person despite what happened. So it upset me last year when I read so much 'dirty washing' coming out in her life story in *Hello!* magazine. It was sad that she had to write it in the first place for financial reasons, but the huge ranch she inherited in the Argentine on Hector's tragic death in 1992 requires a lot of cash to keep it going. What most upset me was that she made out that our marriage had few highlights in it. That is grossly unfair and untrue. During most of the sixteen years we were together, we had a ball. Shooting at Sandringham, dances, parties at Windsor Castle, Ascot week house parties – none of these feature in her memoirs. Susie doesn't describe the fun she had, teaching the children to ride with an unlimited number of horses, or her own hunting and hunters, which she loved. The only polo tour she mentions is the one to the Argentine in 1966. She forgets the tours she went on to South Africa, California, and Chicago. She doesn't mention any of our family holidays abroad, with the exception of one skiing holiday which I didn't go on.

Susie said in her account that she had no idea whether I was going to come back home from Cyprus or not. That was never on the agenda. I could not wait to come back to the children and to her. A dozen large albums, lovingly kept by her, tell the varied story of our marriage, and, in most of the photos, she is smiling. A few, indeed, are in this book.

We were probably too young to have got married in the first place, but if we had communicated with each other more honestly and openly, our marriage would never have ended. I would have stopped any extra-marital dalliances immediately if Susie had told me that she would leave me unless I changed my behaviour. I know I'm not an angel, but my punishment seemed harsh.

Susie and I were finally divorced in May 1974, and she married Hector a year later. I maintained a blind belief in our marriage right up to the day of our divorce, and I called Susie from the divorce court five minutes before I went in.

'If you want,' I said, 'I can stop this right now.'

Then, when it was over, I told her the door was still open if she ever wanted to come back.

I maintained my friendship with Hector. Whenever we met subsequently, on or off the polo field, there was never any animosity between us. I respected him and admired him as a great polo player and a brilliant horseman. The only concession we made to our altered marital status was a gentleman's agreement that we wouldn't umpire each other. This went on for two years, then, at the start of the season after that 'probation', we agreed to carry on as before.

The first match I umpired in which Hector was playing took place during Ascot Week, a medium goal game on the Guards Polo Club's number four ground. Hector was playing against a team organized by Peter Grace. I don't remember who my co-umpire was, but Stuart McKenzie from New Zealand was third man, as referee. Throughout the game, Peter Grace marked Hector closely, as he should have done – he was a three goal player and Hector was a seven. If he could mark closely enough, Hector would soon be out of the game. This was a five chukka match, and in the middle of the fourth chukka, Hector, a strong man, blew his top. With a good right cross he hit Peter Grace and knocked him off his horse. Under such unusual circumstances, my co-umpire and I had no choice but to send him off. The referee agreed and the game went on, with only three players on Hector's side.

Afterwards as I was coming off the ground, Hector came towards me, held out his hand, and said, 'Ronald, you were absolutely right. You had no option. I apologize for my behaviour.'

He was disciplined by the Hurlingham Polo Association and suspended for fourteen days.

As a sequel to all of this, that evening in the club bar two of his Argentinian friends came up to me and said, 'Now you've got your own back, Ronald.' I was very upset. Hector was there, so I went up to him and asked him to sort out his comrades. 'I won't have that sort of rubbish being said,' I added. Both were friends of his, but to give him his due, Hector went over and gave them hell.

CHAPTER TEN

The Monk of Dummer

WITH SUSIE GONE, the first thing I had to do was to ensure my daughters were well looked after. Although they saw her regularly, at fifteen and thirteen they must have missed their mother's day-to-day influence dreadfully. I suppose I was a poor substitute, but I did what I could to stay close to them, and listen to their worries.

At the time of our separation, both Jane and Sarah were attending Hurst Lodge School near Sunningdale, as weekly boarders. Jane left at sixteen and continued her studies at Queensgate College in London, which meant she could live with Susie during the week in Chelsea, and come home to Dummer at weekends.

One unexpected bonus of the separation was that I built up a strong bond with both my daughters, which has remained to this day. In some ways, perhaps, we became too close, even possessive, and it would lead to problems later, when both Jane and I tried to bring other partners into the family. In the meantime, the amount of teasing and ragging that went on at mealtimes had to be seen to be believed. I improved my basic cooking skills and also assumed the role of chaperon and chief censor when it came to boyfriends, weekend parties and music. I played the 'trad Dad' role – bursting into a room full of idle teenagers listening to dreadful music, wondering loudly why no one wanted to do anything out in the fresh air. I developed my nagging skills, and took pains to ensure that Sarah had all her uniform ready for school on Sunday nights.

It must have been difficult for the girls to remain loyal to both parents, to appear even-handed, but neither of them was ever judgemental. I was careful not to speak out against Susie, or force them to take sides.

With Mrs Cole gone, I needed to find another house-keeper, and, after several false starts, I engaged Ros Reynell, a capable girl in her mid-twenties whom the girls took to right away. She was nice, jolly and a marvellous cook, and quickly gained the approval of both grandmothers.

Susie's mother, Grummy, used to spend many weekends at Dummer, and became one of Sarah's greatest confidantes. She would come and do the flowers in the house, and was a regular and welcome visitor right up to her death in 1991. When I remarried, she got on wonderfully well with Sue, making her feel part of the family from the beginning. My mother tells the story that long after the divorce, Grummy insisted on keeping photographs of me on display in her living room, which infuriated Susie. She was a good and loyal friend. When, in later years, adverse publicity used to appear about me, she was on the telephone to my mother right away, offering support. 'What's the silly old thing done now?' she would ask.

Ros Reynell settled in well, taking over some of the dogs that Susie had left behind as well as becoming a great friend of Sarah. What I didn't realize was that some Machiavellian plotting was going on behind the scenes: my mother had decided that Ros would make a suitable second wife, and Ros, in her turn, had begun to agree. I was unaware of this, but later it proved tricky to deal with tactfully. My mother said afterwards that I had been so hurt over the separation and divorce that she was worried I might make a rotten next choice, so she had better do it for me!

I didn't want to know about women at all then. Having experienced the devastation of Susie going, I became totally antisocial. We had had a full social life as a couple; as an individual, I turned into a virtual recluse, and my friend

The Monk of Dummer

Victor Law nicknamed me 'The Monk of Dummer', because I was always refusing his and everybody else's invitations. My life revolved around my daughters. I didn't want to do anything that would make them feel less secure; my place had to be at Dummer for them.

I was still playing polo, but with limited social involvement. I'd play a game, have a drink at the bar, then come straight home. For a long time I didn't feel like accepting any invitations. People were very kind and made constant efforts to get me out of my 'monastery'. There were offers of dinner parties and other social events, but I preferred to stay at Dummer, playing polo, riding horses and generally minding my own business. Later, on the few occasions when I did break out, I made all kinds of feeble excuses to get away early. I spent as little time as possible in London. I wasn't in the mood.

If I had been the chronic womanizer of reputation, this period of my life would surely have been much more colourful. I might have said, 'Whoopee! I'm free!' and rushed around with anyone and everyone, or quickly moved another woman into my life. Instead, the reverse happened. I led a celibate life and didn't even notice other women. My mother's attempts at matchmaking fell on stony ground and I must have been a huge disappointment to her. As time went by, though, the monkishness began to wear off, and I would invite friends down to make up a house party for events such as the local hunt ball. There was never any question of loads of girlfriends. Everything seemed too much effort, and I was worried how the children might react.

Jane and Sarah were at the age when they were capable of being highly critical of anyone new in my life. On more than one occasion they saw someone off whom they didn't like. I had invited a likely girlfriend down to a hunt ball, and she arrived on the Friday at teatime. Just before dinner, Jane took me on one side. 'Daddy,' she said, 'this one's not for you.'

Even though my guest was meant to be staying the weekend, somehow I managed to hustle her back onto a London train the following morning! My daughters' feelings and opinions were of the utmost importance to me. If they didn't like someone, that was it. I had other problems to worry about, anyway, than my own reclusive behaviour. Jane had fallen in love, and I thought she was far, far too young.

The year before she left Dummer, Susie had engaged Binnie Coy, a young Australian girl, to help with her ever-growing stable. In time, Binnie was visited by her cousins Jim and Alex Makim who, like many Australians, were doing the Grand Tour and were on their way to South America. Alex, at seventeen, was a tall blond boy who loved horses and was keen to learn to play polo. When Jim moved on, Alex asked if he could stay to help. To the fourteen-year-old Jane, Alex was the original knight in shining armour, nothing had ever seemed more romantic, and she developed a huge crush on him, much to the amusement of her sister, who teased her mercilessly.

After a few months, Alex rejoined Jim, later returning to Dummer. He was a very useful worker, so I took him on to help with the harvest, and to assist with building a horse corral. Far from being grateful for the experience and the work, Alex soon made it perfectly clear that he disapproved of the way we ran Dummer Down Farm. He was young and arrogant, and believed that we had far too many people working here, compared with the way the Makim family farm was run in Australia. This may have been true, but what he hadn't taken into account was that we ran an entirely different system.

Alex never said so, but I got the impression that he disapproved of me as well. Some of the other farm workers found his rather abrasive manner difficult to tolerate, yet to my eldest daughter he was the most wonderful man in the world. I thought she was too young to become involved in such an intense relationship, and I didn't think she had chosen the right man, either. All this made Alex seem an even more attractive proposition to Jane. I watched helplessly as she demonstrated the same level of obsessive intent over Alex as I had witnessed in her mother over Hector only the year before. I have no doubt that if Susie hadn't left, Jane would have been better able to deal with her emotions. I am sure it was her basic insecurity that drove her into the relationship with Alex, despite all my efforts at trying to keep things normal for her at home.

One possible solution occurred to me: I thought Jane ought to do some travelling. She had led a quiet, sheltered life, and I hoped that if she got away for a few months, she might forget all about this youthful passion. So, when she left Hurst Lodge at the end of the summer term 1973, we arranged for her to go to Kenya for an extended visit. We knew she would be in good hands; her uncle Bryan, Susie's brother, was already living there, and I arranged for her to stay with friends I had met playing polo. I hoped this might be the last I heard of Alex Makim. It was nothing to do with being a possessive Dad – I just did not think he was suitable for her.

That summer of 1973 I made another attempt to escape my monastic behaviour. My good friend Victor Law, with whom I had served in the Life Guards, invited me to a cocktail party. In the crush, wearing a stunning blue silk dress with pink flowers, was one of the most beautiful blondes I had ever seen. Her name was Susan Deptford and she had come with her flatmate Elizabeth Beale, who was also a friend of Victor. Sue knew me slightly by sight; Liz had taken her to various polo matches, and she had enjoyed watching the game. This was enough encouragement for me, and we spent a few moments chatting furiously.

Sue was the first woman who had attracted me since Susie left. I didn't want to let this opportunity pass me by. I summoned up my courage and asked her out for dinner that night. She turned me down. Sue had told her long-time regular boyfriend she would meet him after the cocktail party. I was so downcast by this that it put me back into the monastery for several months and I didn't try to ask anyone out again.

Victor kept saying, 'You must get up to London to meet new people.' To Sue he kept saying, 'I've got this friend down in the country who's really down in the dumps. We must get him to come up and have dinner with us as a foursome. This went on for weeks, trying to arrange a date that was mutually convenient. Finally, on the agreed evening, it was decided that I would come as Sue's date.

First of all, I had to resolve a transport dilemma. I had two cars at the time – a Mercedes 350SL, and the most repulsive pea-green Fiat 127. The Mercedes gobbled up petrol so the hideous Fiat was the one I used as a runaround. Which car should I take to the dinner party at Sue's flat? One was flashy, the other made me seem like a hick. In the end I plumped for the Fiat, which was spotlessly clean inside, but in a diabolical mud-spattered state externally. I was so worried about giving the wrong impression, I didn't use the Mercedes in front of Sue until weeks later.

If first impressions count, the one I received when I reached the foot of the stairs leading up to the Cheyne Walk flat was negative. I loathe garlic – yet the whole place reeked of it, wafting intensely down the stairs. Sue is a trained Cordon Bleu cook who was employed by the Bank of America to cook directors' lunches. That evening she was blithely unaware of my apprehension, and didn't realize until long afterwards the supreme effort I made that night to eat my way through her garlic-laced but wonderful crown roast of lamb. It didn't matter. By that time, I was hooked. I had fallen helplessly in love with her.

Susan Deptford, then twenty-seven, was the daughter of a

successful Norfolk farmer. She been been living in London for about ten years and had a steady boyfriend, but the relationship didn't seem to be going anywhere – and it wasn't something I was going to let stand in my way. The day after the dinner party, I sent her a bunch of red roses with a simple 'WOW' inscribed on the card. She guessed who they were from, and was delighted. Apparently no one had ever sent her flowers before.

Sue told me long afterwards that her flatmate Liz Beale had been very quashing. She had said, 'Don't think anything of it, he's just one of those old-fashioned men who does things like that after a dinner party.' Evidently Sue didn't listen.

Emboldened, I invited Sue and Liz down to stay the weekend to attend the Hampshire hunt ball. It was the first real entertaining I had done since Susie's departure and I made everyone jump through hoops to get the house looking right. Jane was in Kenya, so Sarah was detailed to play hostess, to help choose the menus and make the guests feel at home, and Ros made sure everything was spick and span. I had both grandmothers on hand for support, with Grummy making an extra effort with the flowers. In each of the guest rooms I put a bottle of champagne and an ice bucket, and a card with a funny welcoming message. It must have been obvious how special I thought Sue was, and I was desperately anxious that the weekend should be a success.

It was. Sue fitted into the Dummer situation as if she had been born to it.

'I'd felt so sorry for you,' she told me later. 'You'd painted such a gloomy picture of your life, telling me that you used to sit alone for hours on end with just Mr Bugs [my dog] for company. I imagined you must be living in a huge barren hall. When I arrived, I couldn't believe it, it was so much cosier and warmer than I had imagined.'

A country girl herself, she loved the house, the dogs and the farm, and was especially kind to the teenage Sarah, who was still wary of any new romantic interest in her father's life, and very protective of me.

Sue and I began seeing each other regularly. The polo season was over, so during the week in London we often met for lunch, then went to see a film in the afternoon. Whenever she could she came to Dummer for the weekend. The first time, my mother marched her off to the dining room, sat her down and interrogated her to find out if she might be suitable as a future Mrs Ferguson.

In fact, though I was completely unaware of this, my mother was quite desperate for me to marry Ros, and on many of the weekends when Sue came down, Ros, who could easily have gone off duty, decided to stick around. Ros and Sarah were very close; they had an almost private language, and they excluded Sue from many of their conversations. The situation was complicated for her: she also had to cope with a suspicious Jane, newly returned from Kenya and moping around the house, still missing Alex and feeling thoroughly sorry for herself. Sue handled it all with her customary grace and aplomb; one of her many qualities is patience; another is tact. She soon won the hearts of this regiment of women who were trying to control my life. Sue says I won her heart because she was so touched by the way I handled every detail of my daughters' welfare, trying to be both mother and father.

There was still a fly in the ointment: Sue's regular boy-friend. They had been going out for years in London, and when he realized that Sue was seeing me, he got quite bolshie and started to make life difficult for her.

Christmas 1973 was particularly trying. Sue had gone home to Norfolk. I felt she ought to be there, that it would be wrong for the children if she were at Dummer. I was keen for Jane and Sarah to have the same sort of Christmas as they had when their mother had been here, but this caused conflicting loyalties. I have never regretted giving the girls so much of my attention at that time. I am sure it was the right thing to do. But it must have been hard on Sue, who coped remarkably well. To my shame, I gave her little help. But when her boyfriend began to cause trouble, I could see that I might end up losing her if I wasn't careful. I decided I must act.

Shortly after that awful Christmas we had spent largely apart, I thought I would whisk her away. I had been invited to play polo in California.

'Why not come with me?' I said.

To my profound delight, Sue readily accepted. I put a further plan into action. I made a telephone call to Garrard, the jewellers . . .

In California, we stayed with my friend Michael Butler who was on a bit of a vegetarian kick at the time. Mealtimes consisted of things like boiled dandelions and brown rice, so after a couple of these culinary nightmares, Sue and I got into the habit of filling up on hamburgers and french fries at the local drug store before dinner, knowing all we would get would be tofu soup. It was quite hilarious.

The first night we arrived at Michael's house, we visited some friends of his who had tented Persian drapes all over the room, and lots of candles and incense burning. We sat round in a circle – the atmosphere was weird, not a situation I felt comfortable in. At one point, a strange-looking cigarette was passed from hand to hand. To my relief, when it got to Sue, she declined in her politest, most English way, and passed it straight on. I feel strongly about drugs. If she had taken one puff, I'm sure I would have changed my mind about her. She jokes to this day – if only she had known, she might have been saved!

A few days later, on top of a mountain near Santa Barbara, I asked Sue to be my wife. In my trouser pocket was the ring I had designed and had made for her. Garrard had delivered it, with heart-stopping urgency, directly to me at the airport before we left England, and no one knew anything about it.

We were so excited, we couldn't wait to tell everyone. It was Sunday, and I knew that all my family, including Jane, would be at Dummer, so I decided to telephone and tell them the news. On reflection, this was probably one of my more stupid moves. I was greeted with stunned disbelief. The vibes down the telephone were decidedly hostile; instead of my family leaping about at the prospect of my marrying Sue, they all sounded very low key. They had no idea that our romance – then only about six months old – had progressed this far, and they had had no clue that I wanted to marry her. Rightly or wrongly, the girls, who were particularly possessive at that time, were upset that I had gone ahead and made such an important decision without consulting them first. Ros Reynell had her own reasons for feeling let down, and to a certain extent, the girls sympathized with her. I realized, too late, that I should have waited until we returned, then discussed it with them all face to face. News of this dimension doesn't travel well down the telephone wires.

Poor Sue. On our return, I suggested gently that she took off the ring and didn't wear it until I had smoothed some of the ruffled feathers at Dummer. She admits now that she thought I had gone off the whole idea. She had already telephoned her own parents, who had started making plans for the wedding. 'When will it be?' they kept asking. 'Probably in May, before the polo season begins,' Sue replied confidently.

If only she had known. Undeterred by the lack of a firm date, her mother went ahead and made three tiers of the wedding cake anyway.

Sue isn't a person who creates problems, neither does she go in for hysterical outbursts, but she really had to bring into play every ounce of patience she possessed when we returned from California. Instead of looking forward to her new life with me, she had to stand back and watch me appease the grandmothers, the housekeeper and my two daughters for my thoughtlessness in asking for her hand. I feel quite humble when I look back and realize what she had to put up with.

I still had the problem of my daughter Jane. Having returned from Kenya, she was even more determined that it was Alex she wanted. She couldn't get him out of her head. I thought maybe a short sharp dose of the Australian outback could be the answer. If she was to go ahead with the romance, I reasoned, then she ought to find out exactly what she was in for, how basic her life would be in Australia. Alex Makim was by then farming his own property, Wilga Warrina, in New South Wales, so I allowed her to go out and find out for herself just how rough it was all going to be. She didn't live with Alex, but close by, with Alex's father.

I hoped this would fix things, but of course it had the opposite effect. She worked hard on the farm, and did everything she was asked to do, which was a surprise to me because she had led such a sheltered life. Alex asked her to marry him; I refused to let her get engaged. She came back to England forlorn and lovesick and moped around the house in tears a lot of the time.

'You'll get married before I do,' said Sue to Jane.

'I cannot possibly marry you,' I said to Sue, 'until my own children are sorted out.'

Prophetic words. As it turned out, if we had taken them at face value, we would still be waiting! I was so wrapped up in family matters, so worried about Jane, I don't know how Sue put up with it. Her patience is legendary, something she has certainly had to stretch to the limit throughout her life with me.

In the end, of course, I gave in. This seems to be standard procedure for all fathers when put under enormous pressure from their children. I agreed to Jane marrying Alex, and we planned a July wedding at the pretty twelfth-century Dummer Church, just a month before Jane's eighteenth birthday.

She would be the same age her mother had been when we were married, but twenty years on, our elder daughter still seemed impossibly young.

I was also faced with the almost unthinkable prospect that Jane would end up living in Australia. This is still a huge sadness for me. I am often asked how I feel about Sarah, but Jane is equally my daughter, and if Susie hadn't left her, I am convinced this early marriage would never have taken place. Jane would have married an Englishman, and would still be in this country.

Susie, by now living in the Argentine with Hector, came back specially to help Jane prepare for the wedding, and the house seemed to fill up with women discussing table plans, looking at wedding lists, rejecting dress designs. Not surprisingly, Sue didn't want to add to the chaos, and refused to come down during this period, so our meetings were confined to London. Looking back, at a time when she had hoped to be planning her own wedding, it must have been difficult to have been upstaged by a seventeen-year-old.

Alex's family flew over from Australia and the reception was held in a marquee in the garden at Dummer Down House. I invited Sue to the wedding, but she felt awkward about being there. At the wedding breakfast, she burst into tears when the kindly vicar she was sitting next to politely enquired when her own wedding was to take place.

I put on a brave face and waved my eldest daughter off to Australia, full of misgivings about her future, worried most of all that she would be such a long way away and out of reach if anything were to go wrong.

Life then almost got back to normal. Sue returned to Dummer at weekends, and slowly and surely forged a strong bond with Sarah, my mother and ex-mother-in-law. Despite my tactless piece of timing, they got on marvellously with each other. However, the following year, when I had failed to progress the plans for our own wedding, her patience snapped. I knew I had already stretched it beyond reasonable expectation. I still loved her very much, but I was acting in a rather cowardly fashion, always allowing family demands and pressures to come first. I was worried, too, that our expectations weren't quite the same. Sue wanted children. I felt that with all that I had gone through with Jane, I had quite enough to cope with already. Sue felt it was unfair to both of us to get married under these circumstances, so finally she told me it was over.

'I'm going to move flats, get another job, start a new life,' she said. 'I've put the ring in the bank, we're not getting married, so please don't telephone me or pester me. I'm not even going to tell you where I am, but if anything ever happens to Mr Bugs, please let me know.'

Sue had become very close to my dog during her Dummer visits and was genuinely concerned about his welfare. After a few weeks of separation, completely heartbroken, I ignored her instructions and rang. I knew she was living with her ex-flatmate, Liz, who was now married. Convinced that Mr Bugs had been killed, Sue rushed to the telephone.

'Mr Bugs – what's happened?' she asked.

'Mr Bugs is perfectly all right,' I replied. 'I want to marry you. I have decided I can't live without you.'

'What about children?' she said.

'I can't wait to hear the patter of tiny feet,' I replied. 'There is only one condition. We must get married next week.'

Cautiously, Sue began to come round.

It was an amazing challenge to organize a wedding in a week, but we did it. Sue had already bought her dress from Bellville Sassoon two years previously – her mother thought she would never wear it. The three tiers of wedding cake that had been sitting in the larder in Norfolk for two years had to be quickly transported to London, and we married at Chelsea Register Office on 19 November 1976, with Sue's father, Frederick Deptford, and my mother as witnesses. It was the first and only time I have ever ridden on a London bus. I decided to take the number 19 from Sloane Square to the register office, dressed in all my finery, just for the hell of it.

We had escaped some of the family emotions. Jane was in Australia, and Sarah staying in the Argentine with her mother, so it was a quiet affair, with a blessing at St Paul's, Knightsbridge, afterwards by my friend the Reverend Chad Varah. We had a wonderful lunch party for family and friends at the Berkeley Hotel. Sue had arranged for the menu to include Dummer cream from our dairies and Hungate peas from her own father's farm. Her bouquet included sprays of wheat from both farms, and although the celebrations were held in London, they had a real country style to them. When it was all over, we came back to Dummer.

There never was an official honeymoon, and to this day Sue says she has never had one. Shortly after our wedding, I was off on another polo trip to India. 'You don't want to come,' I said. 'You'd hate it.'

So I went off to India and, as Sue has always said, that was Ronald's honeymoon.

CHAPTER ELEVEN

The International Polo Day

A COMPLETELY new event was added to the English summer sporting scene in 1972. Everyone is familiar with Ascot, Henley and Wimbledon; the International Polo Day has now become as important a date on the calendar. From the beginning it was my 'baby'.

In 1971, a committee was formed to organize the International comprising myself, Lord Patrick Beresford, later to become *chef d'équipe* of the British three-day-event team, and Geoffrey Cross, chairman of the Royal Windsor Horse Show Club. I had already acquired plenty of ideas and a certain showbiz acumen from my experience of taking the Military Tattoo to America, so I just took over in my usual autocratic manner!

The International Day is the major polo event in the country, held on the last Sunday of July. It combines brilliant polo of international standard, plus pomp and ceremony of a style that only this country can produce. Two bands of the Household Division are on parade, complete with drum horse and trumpeters. They play on the smooth green turf of Smith's Lawn before lunch and the match, with all the flags flying in the background. It is the only occasion in the year that the England team plays at Smith's Lawn, against an international team of the same handicap.

When the Prince of Wales decided he wanted to play, a second team and a second match were instituted. The Prince's team was first called Young England, then as he got older and wasn't of a high enough handicap to play in the senior team, his team became known as England 2. Now it's called the Prince of Wales's team.

In 1972 and 1973, I had the dubious distinction of running the day and playing polo as well. In 1973, London Weekend Television hit upon the ingenious idea of fitting me with a microphone so I could play and give a live commentary at the same time. It was the year after Susie had left me, and John Bromley, then head of sport at LWT, says there was a hilarious tape recording, which he swears he's destroyed, of me in full flow, trying to chat up one of the lady guests. My microphone had no off switch, and in the excitement I'd completely forgotten I was wired for sound. Apparently the television control-room boys were all in hysterics! John has since become one of my most trusted friends.

The overall style of the International and its garden party atmosphere made it a must for corporate entertaining. Companies and their guests were accommodated in a tented village on the Smith's Lawn number two ground. Between three and a half and four thousand people would arrive around noon. The luncheon box enclosure was in the shape of a horseshoe. The band played on a bandstand in the centre, which meant people could have drinks outside and listen before going in to lunch. Unlike Ascot, there is no formal dress code and the whole day is delightfully casual, the men in blazers or jackets and ties.

I was severely criticized in 1981 for allowing the Prince of Wales to play. 'What would happen,' the critics said, 'if the Prince was injured and couldn't attend his own wedding?'

At the beginning of May that year, I had taken the precaution of asking him if he would play on International Day, if selected.

'Yes, of course,' he replied. 'Why not?'

I never said another word to him about it, didn't ask him again, but a lot of people told me I should have discouraged him. I have to admit that at the end of that International Day, when the Prince of Wales had played and driven off intact at the end of the game, I felt a great sense of relief.

A huge number of visiting dignitaries had come to London for the Royal Wedding, and it seemed that most of them wanted to attend the International – including Mrs Nancy Reagan. I was summoned to a special security reconnaissance by her Secret Service and our Special Branch, which met at my offices at the Guards Polo Club.

'Of course, Mrs Reagan will arrive with an entourage of about twenty police motor bicycles and cars,' I was told.

'Fine, OK,' I said.

'Now, Major, please give us the details of how Her Majesty the Queen and Prince Philip will arrive so that we can co-ordinate the arrangements,' said the officious American Secret Service man.

I told them that the Queen would probably drive herself in her black Rover with her personal protection officer, and that Prince Philip was likely to drive over from Windsor Castle in his horse and carriage and stop at the Royal Box.

'Don't be so silly, Major,' they replied. 'Get serious.'

I was, and it was exactly what happened. The Queen arrived informally, driving her own car. Prince Philip turned up in a flurry of horses and reins, causing complete traffic chaos for miles. Mrs Nancy Reagan arrived, long after the Queen, in the midst of an enormous entourage of policemen and black Secret Service vehicles. The chairman of the Hurlingham Polo Association, Brigadier Peter Thwaites, and Colonel Richard Watt then came forward to greet her formally, and she was ushered into the Royal Box. There was only one problem. The entire Secret Service wanted to follow, five or six men. I said no, just one. 'The Queen has only her personal protection officer present, so Mrs Reagan needs only one person, too.'

Next, a representative of the White House press corps came to see me. Like the British press, the American press had been kept back to let the VIPs get to their seats.

'Our press aren't treated like this. They've got to go into the Royal Box,' the representative complained.

'Sorry,' I told him, 'they stay out. Nobody else is allowed in.'

About a week later, a friend sent a clipping from the *New York Times* reporting the event, and saying that the press corps had been deeply offended when they were barred from the Royal Box by an arrogant British major.

For the Americans, the whole day was a security nightmare, and it made them distinctly jumpy. For instance, at half-time, the divots thrown up by the horses' hooves are trodden back in by the crowd. This means that all the people on the far side of the ground use the opportunity to come rushing over to get a closer look at the Queen and the royal party. I warned the Secret Service men that this would happen and they looked at me in alarm. I explained that we created a cordoned-off area well away from the Royal Box. The faces of the Secret Service men were a picture when, at half-time, about a thousand people came stampeding across the ground, pushing and shoving each other in order to get to the front. My view was that what was good enough for the Queen was good enough for Mrs Reagan.

An enormous amount of detail had to be worked out carefully for the day to run smoothly. For example, the provision of enough portable lavatories – 'honeywagons', we called them. I'll never forget one occasion at noon on the Sunday of the International with approximately twenty thousand people about to turn up (numbers grew substantially from year to year), one of the ladies' loo attendants came rushing towards me in a state of some alarm.

'Are you aware that the honeywagon people have failed to put any paper into any of the lavatory cubicles?'

I turned to the International's efficient young secretary. 'Go out and get four hundred loo rolls and don't come back until you've got them.'

'On a Sunday?' She looked at me in amazement. 'Where do I start?'

'Go to the Royal Berkshire and the Berystede.' These were two of the best local hotels. 'Get hold of their house-keepers. Explain the problem, and say we'll replace their loo rolls tomorrow.' Sure enough, twenty minutes later she was back, hundreds of loo rolls piled into the back of her car. Among the excellent secretaries who had helped to organize the day, tribute must be paid to Annabel Dunant, Mary Anne Penno and Celia Medley.

Work on the following year's International always began with a debrief the day after the event. It would simmer quietly through the winter, then take off from April, with all the advance publicity to be done, and tickets to be sold. Over the years, we had relatively few accidents, although the one year that the International was televised live, one of our polo team nearly had his ear cut off during the match. He was filmed in glorious colour, going up for the presentation swathed in blood-soaked bandages. Unfortunately, that part of the proceedings was totally beyond my control!

Some members of the Guards Polo Club saw the International as one huge ego trip for me. But I was keen to point out to my critics that as a result of the success of the day, the sponsors knew how well the Guards Polo Club was run, and it was important to keep the Club's profile high to get the sponsors in.

After I had left the Guards Polo Club, I was bitterly disappointed to see how standards slipped in the organization of the International. Though I was no longer part of it, I still felt personally responsible. I put my criticisms in writing, which only served to heap more trouble on my head. I wrote to both the Hurlingham Polo Association and the Guards Polo Club on Royal County of Berkshire Polo Club headed paper. This was a mistake. My boss, Bryan Morrison, had to distance himself from my attack. I very much regret any embarrassment I may have caused him. I was hopping mad and showed it, but I acted too hastily, without thinking through the consequences.

CHAPTER TWELVE

A New Family

SUE AND I were married in November 1976, and a relatively saga-free period of our lives followed. At first Sue found our way of life quite different from the way she had been brought up. She recalls that her sister and she never argued, her childhood had been peaceful and calm, and her parents, married for fifty years, secured a solid background of traditional values. What a difference, then, to enter into the Ferguson family full of assertive women, where strong personalities would regularly shout at each other and storm out. Little could she have known, in those early days, just what she was embarking on, the second wife of a man whose two daughters were very particular as to whom their father was with. She didn't have the pleasure of choosing her new married home – instead, she inherited a house that had been run by my former wife and had belonged to my mother before that.

Sue was told that she couldn't change a thing unless it was to take down the odd picture. She wasn't even allowed to alter where the saucepans were stored in the kitchen in case it made Jane or Sarah feel insecure. It must have been an awful introduction to married life. To her great credit, her generous nature allowed her to overcome these obstacles. She never made scenes; she showed enormous strength of character, and a determination to make things work.

With Jane in Australia, my immediate responsibilities were to help Sarah decide what she wanted to do with her life. She had spent six months in the Argentine with her mother and

Hector, and initially found it difficult to readjust to life back in London. She settled into a flat with her cousin Ros Bowie and enrolled in a nine-month secretarial course at Queens College in South Kensington. She lived for evenings and weekends; she had a huge social circle and began to enjoy life on the young singles' circuit.

Travel was still on the agenda. In the summer of 1977, she spent a fantastic holiday in the United States with her former schoolfriend Clare Wentworth Stanley at their family home in Nantucket. Back in London, she began going out with her first serious boyfriend, Kim Smith Bingham, who was a couple of years older and worked in the City. Sarah had first met him in South America where he had been working as a ranch hand. The relationship was fairly volatile: I played agony uncle down the telephone line on several occasions: 'Why hasn't he rung? What do you think is going on, Dads?'

Having seen my first daughter marry so young, I had no wish to repeat the experience with the second. I was worried that Sarah and Kim were becoming too involved. As Sarah was still only nineteen, it was time to do some more travelling, in time-honoured Ferguson tradition. To cool things down a bit, we would make a trip to Australia to visit her sister Jane, whose twenty-first birthday had fallen that August. Sue and I were expecting our first child in early September, and it was Sue who suggested that I took Sarah off to Australia soon afterwards – partly to get me out of the way, I suspect.

Needless to say, Sarah didn't forget about Kim, but we had an exciting – if not exactly comfortable – time in Australia. Jane and Alex lived in the middle of nowhere, close to the border of New South Wales with Queensland; the nearest town, North Star, was almost twenty miles away. All it contained was a few houses, one shop and what seemed like about fifteen pubs.

Alex Makim's farm was called Wilga Warrina, which

means 'house among the trees' in Aborigine. It was basic – an L-shaped wooden house with a tin roof, not much more than a shack, set in roughly eight thousand acres of flat, fairly scrubby bush. The temperature in summer would regularly top 100°F. Everything was covered in red dust which turned into a disgusting mire when it rained; the tin roof leaked badly; bowls and buckets to catch the drips were part of the furniture. I had to keep moving my bed around my room to avoid the flood. Telephone wires, chewed by animals, trailed over the floor, and the furniture was plain and battered. The one loo, known as the 'dunny', was outside, to be approached with extreme caution, for you never knew what creepy-crawlies would be waiting for you out there.

Jane's kitchen was worse than basic; it seemed to me to be a health risk.

'I'd like to give Jane a new kitchen,' I told Alex, 'as a present from me.'

Alex frowned. 'It's been good enough for my father and my family, so it's good enough for Jane.'

It would have made no difference if I had paid for and organized everything – he just would not accept it.

Alex didn't approve of the life I led, so he tried to bully me by making me get up every morning at five a.m. to do the rough work around the farm. I knew he hoped to show me up as a useless, over-indulged Pom so I just got on with it – I wasn't going to let Alex get the better of me. Whatever he threw at me, I'd been through worse during my army days; he had seriously underestimated me. The Ronald Ferguson he thought he saw was not me at all.

One morning, Jane sent us to North Star to get provisions. As we drove out of the estate gates – a ramshackle old wire construction – we whooped for joy and relief. It felt as though we were being released from jail. We could have done the shopping in half an hour, but we made it last five hours. Alex had insisted that we ate margarine on the farm, so Sarah and I stocked up with butter, and cow's milk to replace the goats' milk we'd been presented with each day. The two weeks we spent at Wilga Warrina were two of the longest of my life.

We did celebrate Jane's birthday – belatedly, but in some style – with three hundred friends of Jane and Alex's arriving from all over the country – travelling huge distances to a party is the norm over there. When I got up in the middle of the night to visit the dunny, I discovered on my return that my bed had been commandeered by a couple of late revellers. Indeed, the bodies of partygoers too drunk to make it home were draped all over the house.

Having been in Australia for over two years, Jane had settled down and got used to living rough and I suppose she thought she was happy. She put a brave face on it and worked hard. I was proud of her. Before going out to Australia, she had never even been camping. When we left, it must have been hard for her to wave goodbye.

To give Alex his due, he worked all hours of the day and night. He has a mixed farm of cattle, sheep and cereals; but this type of Australian farming is tough. I could never take to it, although I love the outback and get on well with Australians, whose direct approach I like. I got on particularly well with Alex's father, Wilga, who is a good farmer and a hard worker like his son.

I was excited to return to be reunited with my newborn son. On 7 September 1978, my son, Andrew Frederick John, had been born, three weeks before we went to Australia, at the Royal Hampshire County Hospital in Winchester.

When I had first asked Sue to marry me, I wasn't keen to have more children; subsequently I embraced the idea of relatively late second fatherhood with alacrity. When Andrew came along I couldn't have been happier. A lot of people thought it was because he was a boy. This was a thrill, certainly, but more important was that mother and child were safe and well. Having gone through that third, sad pregnancy with Susie, naturally I was apprehensive. After two daughters, it was a marvellous experience to have a son, but not, as for some men, to further my male ego. Isn't it marvellous, people said, now that you can play cricket, golf, tennis and ride with Andrew? Of course it's fantastic, I replied, but I could have done all those things if he'd been a girl.

My third daughter, Alice, was born in Winchester on Boxing Day 1980, just over two years after Andrew. Sue reminds me that, having originally agreed to have more children, I only gave official permission for our first. The others, she says, she had to sneak in.

Five years later Eliza arrived. Sue and I had hoped that she would be born on 10 October, which would have made a hat-trick with my birthday and that of my father. Eliza was induced because I was going to Australia with the Prince of Wales, and I wanted to be sure that both mother and baby were doing well before I left. So Eliza made her entrance into the world at around 4 a.m. on 9 October 1985. I'm convinced that if she had not been induced, she would have been born on the 10th. Sue had Eliza at Basingstoke General Hospital, on the National Health, and hers was the only birth I witnessed.

When Jane and Sarah were born it wasn't the done thing for the father to be in the delivery room. The question didn't arise for either Andrew or Alice, but I did want to be there for Eliza. I knew, at the age of almost fifty-four, that she would be my last child, and it seemed special. I can't say I enjoyed it – I hate the smell and atmosphere of hospitals, but it was a moving and emotional moment when she was born.

When the children were little, we employed local girls as mother's helps for Sue – first Linda, daughter of a neighbouring farmer, who rode in the carriage with Andrew and Alice when they were pageboy and bridesmaid at Sarah's wedding. Then came Mary, daughter of the late Sir James Scott's stud groom. Our third helper, Alison, came as an extra pair of hands during the chaotic wedding year, and stayed on until she married three years ago. All were excellent, and helped contribute to the atmosphere of warmth and stability at home that is so important for children growing up. We don't have any domestic help in the house now, except for the wonderful Mrs Brown who has cleaned the house for over twenty years.

I admit that I'm a much better father the second time around. For a start, I'm at home all the time; when Jane and Sarah were growing up, I was either away soldiering or off on polo trips abroad. Since I left the polo world, Sue and I have a much more even-handed partnership in child-rearing. When Sue's involved in her business and unable to be home after school, I'll be in the kitchen at four p.m., cooking the kind of tea that I hope will earn an eight-year-old's approval. Lack of culinary expertise is sternly criticized, although my sausages are occasionally highly praised!

I've always enjoyed reading bedtime stories to the children. My all-time favourite, with no apologies whatsoever, is *Little Black Sambo*; I also love the perennial childhood classics such as the *Just So Stories*, *The House at Pooh Corner* and *The Wind in the Willows*. I've read to the younger ones all the books read to Sarah and Jane but they loved it best when I made up stories and Andrew asked for them 'coming out of my ears'. I love taking the children to pantomimes, and I still play tricks on the family, never revealing the location of the treat until the last minute.

Andrew did much better than me at Ludgrove (this wouldn't have been hard!), and was always happy there. To my joy, he passed with ease the common entrance exams to Eton, where the standard is much higher now than it was in my day. Andrew is a strong well-made boy who is keen on sport. He has been captain of his rugger team for two halves. He plays water polo and golf, as well as rowing and playing cricket. What is more, unlike his father, he appears to be holding his own academically.

At fifteen, naturally he is undecided about what he wants to do in life. I'm not exerting any pressure on him, although I'd love him to become another Ferguson in the Life Guards. I believe that military discipline when you're young stands you in good stead for the rest of your life. Recently, Andrew has taken a big interest in the farm and is out with the foreman most days when he's at home. He's also close to his maternal grandfather who runs a large intensive farm in Norfolk, and enjoys spending time with him there.

Andrew rides well and has further developed his skills through the local pony club. He'll be too big and heavy to compete in point-to-points – he's far bigger boned than I was. He won't have to live under my shadow on the polo ground either, because he's left-handed. When he was about eleven, he tried polo but found it impractical to hold the stick in his right hand. In a way, it's a relief. The way that polo has changed in this country means I wouldn't want him to participate anyhow.

Alice, at thirteen, is a tall, athletic girl with much of her mother's looks and grace. She decided that she wanted to go to boarding school, and she's at North Foreland Lodge, the other side of Basingstoke, where she is head of her form and appears to be very popular and happy. Her recent school reports are all excellent. She is a splendid companion, great fun and very loving. She's a good swimmer, plays tennis whenever she can, and is marvellously co-operative about the house. She rides extremely well, with the necessary guts, and has recently started to take local pony events seriously. However, on an outing to a London go-kart track, Alice beat everyone hands down.

The boys made excuses afterwards. 'Alice got in the way,' they complained.

'Alice didn't get in the way,' I replied. 'She was half a lap ahead of you all.'

Eliza was the most marvellous baby. Her birth was swiftly succeeded by the announcement of Sarah's engagement and the Royal Wedding, so in the first year of her life, she wasn't exactly overburdened with attention. She sailed sweetly through it all, charming everyone with her sunny nature. She is doing well at Daneshill School and is probably ahead of the other two, academically, at the same age.

I go with the children to their pony club events, hunter trials and show jumping competitions and I try to give them as much help and support as I can. I'm no expert in show jumping, but I try to point out their mistakes. When they finish, I'm relieved and delighted to see them come back in one piece. It would be a bonus if they won a place, but so long as they've enjoyed themselves and the horse has gone well, that's good enough for me. Instinctively, I've taken the same line as my father – if they seriously want to do something, I will give them all the encouragement I can muster. For example, I don't agree with hunting these days, but if my children want to do it, I won't stand in their way.

I try never to miss a school match, whether Alice is playing netball or lacrosse, or Andrew is playing rugger or football. They've certainly been dragged along to polo often enough! They are all pretty competitive, like me. At home, from time to time I ban television, and we all play games like Monopoly and Racing Demon. Eliza usually wins, either because she cheats or she's more skilful than the rest of us. None of us is sure which it is.

All the children adore animals. We have three Jack Russells in the house, Bella, Bramble and Biggles – a far more effective early-warning system than any burglar alarm: they start a cacophony of barking long before a stranger has even set foot on the drive. Bella, the oldest, is mine, Bramble, who is Bella's daughter, thinks she belongs to Andrew, and Alice has adopted Biggles.

I like to think that my younger children have had a happy

upbringing. When scurrilous things have appeared about me in the press, I've talked to the children about them. Most importantly, I want them to understand that Sue and I are always here for them. On several occasions, we've had to emphasize that they have no need to be concerned or worried. Children can be incredibly cruel, although I don't think mine have suffered too badly from what others may have said.

Sue, on the other hand, had to go through hell when the newspapers decided to 'expose' me. It is an understatement to say that she has been the most incredibly loyal wife. She is placid by nature and possesses a true inner calm which has helped her to surmount the difficulties, yet I know there have been times when she has been near to despair. Throughout everything, Sue has cared for our children with love and dedication, and brought them up to be considerate of others and to have impeccable manners. She has tried not to let outside events impinge on their right to a happy childhood – and she has succeeded admirably.

Blessed with healthy children, Sue felt she wanted to give something back in return. She has worked tirelessly for the general committee of the charity Wellbeing (formerly Birthright), and started up the local Basingstoke branch. She will do anything she can to help other people, sometimes to her own detriment. With all the problems that I have created, all the apparent scandal and the resulting publicity, I am amazed and thankful that Sue is here at all. She has suffered a great deal of personal anguish. Yet, despite the reams of rubbish written about the state of Sue's mind, and the endless speculation on my 'womanizing', there has never been any question of our marriage ending. After seventeen years, I am still bowled over by Sue's creativity and style, and eternally grateful for the warmth, generosity and love that she has brought into my life. In this respect, I am an incredibly lucky man.

Sometimes I'm asked if it's difficult being an older father, but I don't think about my age. I lead a very active life – more so than a lot of younger fathers. What I do wonder is whether, in twenty years' time, say, when Eliza gets married, I will be able to take her down the aisle. She could be twenty-six and I would be eighty. I'm determined to try to make it – if only on my Zimmer frame, or in an electric wheelchair like Grandfather's!

CHAPTER THIRTEEN

A Royal Romance

IN THE SPRING of 1985, Sarah rang me from her London flat in a state of high excitement. She had just heard that she was on the guest list for the Queen's forthcoming Royal Ascot house party. Since our trip to Australia, Sarah had settled down to a typical London single's life. She had found a permanent base in London – a flat in Lavender Gardens, Clapham – which she shared with Carolyn Beckwith-Smith, an old school friend whose mother was also a great friend of Susie's. She was working for a publisher of fine art books called Richard Burton, whom she had met through her boyfriend Paddy McNally. The job was relatively well paid and she loved it.

Prior to that, she had been working for Durden-Smith Communications, a public relations company with offices in Knightsbridge. I knew one of the partners, Neil Durden-Smith, extremely well. He is married to Judith Chalmers, and I had first met him when he was a sports' commentator for the BBC. Through our mutual connections in public relations, we had kept in touch over the years.

Sarah did well in PR; she has a natural ability to remember names and people, to make a client feel that nothing was too much trouble.

'She's got tremendous stamina,' Neil Durden-Smith told me. 'I call her my party star.'

I was pleased and proud that my lively daughter had grown into such an attractive and independent young woman, and was making a success of her life. On weekends when she wasn't off partying somewhere, she'd come home to Dummer. She loved to help out with baby Andrew, for she and Sue had by this time developed a close and caring relationship. They gossiped about London life and Sarah's boyfriends, providing a link for Sue between domesticity and the London scene she had left behind. Sarah's grandmothers, whom she saw regularly, also provided emotional and moral support whenever it was needed.

Sarah's arrival at Dummer was accompanied by a huge bag of dirty washing. Even when she couldn't make it home for the weekend, her washing did. She would send it down to Basingstoke station by Red Star on a Friday evening and ask us to collect it.

'I'll be calling in on Sunday night on my way back to London,' she'd say. 'Can I pick it up then?'

I used to joke that I'd arrive at the station and there would be Sarah's washing, running down the platform to meet me.

For her twenty-first birthday, I had given a cocktail party for a hundred and fifty guests at the Berkeley Hotel. I'd offered her a dance at Dummer, but she refused, saying she would rather have the money for the next trip she had planned. Shortly after her birthday, Sarah was off travelling again, back to South America with her friend Charlotte Eden to visit Susie and Hector at their new ranch at El Pucara. From there, they travelled on through South America down to Rio, then to the Rocky Mountains to ski at Squaw Valley, before coming back through America via Palm Springs and Louisiana. They were away for almost six months, during which time Alice had been born, and Sue telephoned Sarah asking her to be Alice's godmother.

At the time of the royal invitation, Sarah was working hard, partying hard, and involved in what had been a fairly lengthy and intense relationship with Paddy McNally. She had met Paddy in Switzerland, where he had a house in Verbier. Sarah first started going to Verbier to visit Kim Smith Bingham, who had taken a seasonal job in the ski shop. When things started to go wrong with Kim, Sarah turned to Paddy for comfort. He was twenty-two years older than her, a former racing driver turned businessman, and they began a love affair which lasted three years. I was always concerned for Sarah, but never worried. She was having fun and enjoying herself, so why should I be? Unlike Jane, Sarah was fairly streetwise and could look after herself. Although there were times when she would discuss aspects of her private life with me, I never asked questions. I believe that if someone wants to tell me something, then they will.

Sarah spent a lot of time with Paddy in Verbier. Paddy's wife had died of cancer. Although he had been separated from her before her death, he was certainly in no hurry to remarry. It seemed to Sue and me that Sarah wanted something more permanent than what was on offer. She has never been someone who takes relationships casually. She had also grown extremely fond of Paddy's two young sons, Sean and Rollo, and they of her. Yet I always suspected that things weren't going to work out the way she had hoped.

Sarah was part of a social set in London that included the Princess of Wales. She had become friendly with Diana, and had been a guest at her wedding to Prince Charles in 1981. I never knew much about this friendship, only that they were close, and it was Diana who engineered the invitation to Royal Ascot. The Queen has always enjoyed the company of younger people, and she certainly would have sought her daughter-in-law's help when drawing up her guest list. So the invitation wasn't exactly a bolt out of the blue, although it was a wonderful surprise – a chance for the next generation of Fergusons to socialize with the younger generation of the Royal Family.

During the days of my polo-playing friendship with Prince Philip, Susie and I had been invited to make up the Ascot house party on more than one occasion. Sarah had friends who had already been, so between us we were able to give her some advice as to what would happen and what would be expected of her. The routine at Windsor for Ascot is fairly simple. In the mornings, you can go for a ride with the rest of the house party and gallop up to the race course, you can go and play golf at a nearby course; or you can be taken on a guided tour of some of the art treasures in Windsor Castle, which Susie did one year and thoroughly enjoyed.

When I had stayed at Windsor Castle, I would rush off to play polo after the racing, much to Susie's consternation. If I then played a second game, I was left with only about fifteen minutes to get dressed for dinner, which at the Castle in those days meant white tie. Fortunately, the Queen knew about these sporting commitments, and was very understanding. I don't think I was ever actually late for dinner, but quite frequently, despite having bathed, I would still be sweating quietly from my exertions on the polo field as we joined the Queen for pre-dinner drinks.

After lunch at the Castle, the royal party leaves for the racecourse in a convoy of cars. The middle of Windsor Great Park is the changeover point, where the Queen's guests go from the cars into the open-topped carriages for the rest of the short journey to the course. In 1985, I went along to see my daughter make this début. I fell in with the crowds who always assemble at the car changeover point to get a closer view of the royals, but I stood well back, hidden behind some trees. From there, I had a clear vantage point so I could watch Sarah alight from one of the gleaming black limousines. Dressed in her much-discussed finery, she gaily stepped into one of the open-topped carriages accompanied by other royal guests. For a proud father, it was truly a wonderful moment; little did I know then that the following year, it would be the Queen Mother's carriage that Sarah would be joining.

By all accounts, the romance between my daughter and Prince Andrew began that Ascot week. I heard that she had sat next to him at lunch, and there had been a great deal of banter between them when he tried to force her to eat chocolate profiteroles. It was certainly not the first time they had met. That had happened some years earlier on the polo ground, and they had been vaguely aware of each other's existence since. Through polo, my family had grown up in the shadow of the Royal Family, so none of this was entirely new or unexpected for Sarah.

Sarah began to meet Andrew afterwards, but I didn't hear any of the details; she played her cards close to her chest and news of any romance was low key. Certainly, throughout that summer, Paddy McNally was still on the scene, and it wasn't until she finally split with him in the autumn that it dawned on us that things might be serious between Sarah and Prince Andrew. As a serving naval officer, he was often away at sea, and when Sarah was staying alone with us at Dummer, he would ring her from wherever he was in the world, which was terribly exciting. If he didn't ring, Sarah would want to know why, and it was Sue, not I, who shouldered the burden of the 'why hasn't he rung me?' confidences.

I knew then that things were beginning to escalate. I didn't ask any questions, I just felt it. She talked to Sue about it more than she did to me, but there were times when she would talk to both of us about what she was doing, where she was going. I again took the attitude that she would tell me only what she wanted to. Although we had been close, she did not confide in me much at this time. Those first few months, however, it was clear that Sarah was happy. She was in love, and there were none of the dramas that had accompanied her previous relationships.

I suppose I was somewhat blasé about the situation. I was concerned about Sarah's happiness more than anything else. When it occurred to me that she might end up marrying him, it was the man himself who interested me, not that he was the Queen's son. Uppermost in my mind was the question: is he good enough for her? I was an acquaintance of his father and I liked his brother, but I hardly knew Prince Andrew – although I felt I knew him because I had read and seen so much about him.

Andrew had acquired quite a reputation as a ladies' man, for which I was rather relieved. He was a normal young sailor who had had a string of girlfriends; it all seemed very healthy as far as I was concerned. Sarah and Andrew were just two young people falling in love with each other. I certainly did not sit around day and night thinking about Sarah and what she was doing, neither did I ring her endlessly and ask what was going on. Much of the time, I would have to read about her activities in the newspapers before she got round to telling me herself.

The tabloids got wind of the romance in a big way that Christmas. Sarah was here at Dummer, and this was the first time we experienced the siege of reporters and cameramen that would become a constant in our lives. Sarah wasn't going to say anything about the relationship, and neither was I. Reporters and cameramen crept about the bushes day and night and we found it very tedious to have our privacy invaded in this fashion. It was the first time I had come up against this directly, although I had been involved with the press through Prince Charles. My attitude to them then had been 'mind your own business', but now I realized it was no good taking that stance. At the same time, I wasn't marching to the bottom of the drive to talk to them, either.

That Christmas was a taste of things to come. Press interest and speculation curtailed Sarah's activities alarmingly – no longer could she just drive down to the village shop, or go off on her own when she liked. Wherever she went, she was followed. She wanted to get on with her own life, as did we all, but from that moment, our lives were under the microscope. Up until then, her relationship with Prince Andrew had been as one ordinary person going out with another. We were realistic enough to know that this 'ordinariness' would come to a blinding halt sooner or later because of who he was.

Sarah was warmly welcomed by the Royal Family when she was invited to spend New Year with them at Sandringham. When she returned to Lavender Gardens a posse of reporters and cameramen awaited her. It was the same outside Richard Burton's offices in Hanover Square. In February, she joined the Prince and Princess of Wales on a skiing holiday in Klosters, which was all part of being brought into the family. Then, when Andrew's ship HMS *Brazen* docked in the port of London, she and Diana took Prince William aboard to meet him. Clearly the relationship was serious, and media attention and speculation grew in proportion. The weekend of 23 February, Sarah flew to Newcastle-upon-Tyne under an assumed name to join Prince Andrew at Floors Castle, home of the Duke and Duchess of Roxburghe. There, he asked her to marry him.

The proposal was a complete surprise, although by then the romance was so well established that she must have thought it was a possibility. By all accounts, she was so shocked – and this is typical of Sarah – that she gave him the chance to retract the following morning. I have been asked if Sarah discussed with me the possibility of her marrying into the Royal Family; I don't recall that she ever did. At twenty-six, she was certainly old enough to make her own decisions about her future. In any case, I was hardly going to say no.

It was a very excited Sarah who rang home to Dummer on that Sunday morning. 'Dads, he's asked me to marry him,' she said. 'We can't tell anyone officially yet – but I wanted to tell you.'

'That's fantastic, marvellous, many, many congratulations.'

We were all delighted for her, not, as you might imagine, because he was a prince and the Queen's second son, but because she was so overwhelmingly happy. News of the engagement had to be kept secret for nearly three weeks, because the Queen and Prince Philip were on a tour of Australia and New Zealand and Andrew had to ask his mother for formal permission. In the meantime, he had a discussion with me. He rang me at home one evening.

'I want to talk to you about something,' he said.

'Fine,' I said. 'Where do you want to meet?'

I already knew this would happen, because Sarah had warned me, but I didn't let on that I knew.

'Are you at the Castle?' I asked him. He was. 'Why don't we meet in the Park?'

At 12.20 p.m. that day, I left my office at the Guards Polo Club and drove the five minute journey to meet Prince Andrew at the end of the Long Walk, just below the copper horse.

'I just thought I ought to see you,' he said. 'I want to marry your daughter. What do you think about that?'

'Fantastic,' was all I said. I shook his hand. 'Many congratulations. I'm truly delighted.'

There was nothing else to be said. It was hardly likely, after all, that I was going to ask him what his prospects were or whether he could keep my daughter in the manner to which she was accustomed. From my point of view, my daughter had just become engaged to a man I hardly knew. Normally, with a potential son-in-law, your daughter would bring him down to stay, but Prince Andrew was in a different category. Later, when I did get to know him, I really liked him, and still do to this day.

The engagement was announced, and I wrote to the Queen to say how pleased I was. When I accompanied Prince Charles on his tour of Australia, we had only a brief discussion about it. We were there to play a game, and we got on with it. As I have already mentioned, Prince Charles and I did not discuss personal matters. In any case, there was never time – he was always late for everything.

One important discussion that I now needed to have with my daughter was how her life was going to change. It had already been decided that immediately prior to the announcement of the engagement, Sarah would move into rooms in Buckingham Palace. The situation with the media at Lavender Gardens was already impossible, and would become even more so. This in itself was quite a big step. Imagine – one day you're living happily in Clapham with a flatmate, the next you're in Buckingham Palace.

From the knowledge that I had of the Royal Family, I tried to explain to Sarah how she would no longer be a private person. She had heard this before, of course, particularly from the Princess of Wales, but there is a big difference between being told that your private life is going to be taken away from you, and actually experiencing it. When you're in love, you think it will conquer all. Sarah was well aware of the pitfalls, but she thought that her vitality and strength would enable her to see it through. I had no misgivings either; I thought that Sarah would be able to handle the adversities and problems which marrying into that family would bring. I had been on a couple of royal tours with the Prince of Wales, so I knew about the restrictions, and that Sarah wouldn't be able to go anywhere again without the eyes of the world on her. I thought she would be strong enough to cope with it, and that she would bring a breath of fresh air to the House of Windsor – as did a lot of people in those early, happier days.

Sarah got on well with the Queen. She still does. They share a love of horses and the countryside, and Sarah's natural warmth and charm soon endeared her to the slightly more guarded members of the Royal Family. After the success of Diana, four years earlier, they hoped that the introduction of Sarah would further increase their credibility, particularly with the younger generation. The tabloids went wild, producing acres of print, publishing every tiny detail they could find about Sarah, our family and background. When the press called her the 'Milkmaid from Dummer', my mother thought it was funny. But when they referred to Sarah as a 'middle-class farmer's daughter', my mother went into a frenzy of rage.

The engagement was formally announced on Wednesday, 19 March, which just happened to be the day I was flying to Australia. I had made a commitment several months earlier to be a judge at the Sydney Royal Easter Horse Show, and to see Jane. I was also looking forward very much to seeing my granddaughter, Ayesha, who had been born the previous year. Jane had suffered two miscarriages and the tragic death of another daughter, Florida, at just one day old. Along with the pleasure and excitement of Sarah's burgeoning romance, during those months there had also been the terrible sadness of being thousands of miles away from my Jane.

A lot of people thought I was mad to go to Australia on the day the engagement was announced. I saw no reason to stay; I already had a prior commitment, it was Sarah and Andrew's day, so why hang around? What was I needed for? I was mindful of Jane, who had arranged the trip, and who obviously needed me. Of course, the village of Dummer was besieged, and so was our house, but Sue coped brilliantly, saying that she was very happy.

Four days after I arrived in Australia, having got through a press conference and been more or less left alone to get on with the job in hand, Sarah rang with more news. The date for the wedding had been set – Wednesday, 23 July. I groaned in horror. 'Thanks a lot,' I said. 'That's a terrific day. It also happens to be four days before the International Day, when I have over twenty thousand guests arriving.'

'Dads, you can do it.'

'OK, fine.' That was just the beginning. I was naïve enough to think that I would be able to get on with my own life, that it wouldn't change at all.

How wrong I was.

CHAPTER FOURTEEN

Wedding Bells

TO THE AUSTRALIANS, it was quite something to discover that the sister of Prince Andrew's new fiancée was alive and well and living in their midst. That March in Sydney, Jane had come down to join me at the Easter Horse Show, and we found ourselves thrown into the media glare amid celebrations for the forthcoming wedding. For Jane, this was fairly enjoyable to begin with: it meant that a fraction of the limelight surrounding her sister was reflected on her.

It was wonderful to see Jane and the grandchildren, although I suspected that all was not entirely rosy within the Makim marriage. I kept my own counsel. I had big enough headaches with another marriage looming on the horizon. Jane and I decided that when she and Alex came over to England for Sarah's wedding, we would have little Ayesha christened in Dummer Church the preceding week.

Sarah tried to go on with a normal life from her suite in Buckingham Palace. She continued to work for her publishing house, but the minute she stepped outside the Palace, she was gazed at and judged. It was much the same within the Palace walls. I had told Sarah that never again would she be able to be a private person, but I don't think she knew what would happen until she experienced it first hand. She couldn't wander around in her dirty old jeans any more, wearing no make-up. With all the flunkeys and hangers-on around the Palace, she had to present herself properly at all times, to pay attention to what she said and whom she saw.

Despite her long talks with the Princess of Wales about what it would be like, the reality came as a shock. She was always being observed and judged as a prospective member of the Royal Family. Although she managed superbly, Sarah, who is happiest in casual clothes, found those early days quite a strain. Buckingham Palace isn't a private place; all the rooms lead off corridors, there are no private entrances to apartments, and because so much of the building is offices, there's a bustling atmosphere, with masses of people milling about.

Being accepted by the Royal Family had been one thing. Gaining the approval of the ranks of people who surrounded them was quite another. This was the first time Sarah had encountered the senior Palace courtiers, the people I call the toadies. They gossip between themselves all the time. There's much back-biting and criticism. Most of them are more snobbish than even the most aloof member of the Royal Family, so I've always kept out of their way. I've dealt with Prince Charles's lot, but I didn't know Andrew's at all.

Sarah was trying to be herself, which, of course, didn't enhance her status with these toadies. They're not used to it. They'd react pompously, showing their disapproval by being cool and distant towards her. This was painful for Sarah, who like most of us wants people to like her. Perhaps those early days should have served as a warning. She should have realized that she would no longer be able to be her normal self – spontaneous and impulsive.

I was known on the various gates into the Palace, so I was able to go and see her regularly, and we would meet during the day if I had a couple of hours free in London. We discussed the restrictions that were beginning to haunt her, and I tried to help her adjust her attitude. When she became aware that people were criticizing what she wore, she had to step up her fashion sense, with advice from those inside the Palace and from the Princess of Wales. She did make a big effort to smarten up, although there were some colossal mistakes with some of her outfits. Little did she realize that the Killer Bimbos of Fleet Street were already marking her card. My own life was fairly full, juggling playing polo, acting as Polo Manager to the Prince of Wales and doing my job as chairman of the Guards Polo Club all at the same time. Being Sarah's father didn't change my life – but the glare of publicity intensified.

A lot of interview requests came in. I never took advice as to which I should do; I decided to pick and choose, but limit the number. I didn't want my work affected by journalists coming to interview me at the Guards Polo Club and upsetting the equilibrium there. I was determined that Sarah's new life and her forthcoming wedding should not interfere with my own work. The build-up to the International Day was gathering momentum and there was a colossal amount to be done.

For a royal wedding, all the invitations are issued on behalf of the Queen by the Lord Chamberlain, and the whole occasion is paid for by the Queen and the State. With so many official dignitaries who had to be asked, plus all of Andrew's personal friends, Sarah was only allowed to invite a very few guests in her own right. A certain number of important members of our family were not invited. Understandably it caused great offence at the time, and my mother was very upset. Matters were made worse when we found out that showbusiness friends of Andrew's, such as Elton John and Billy Connolly, had been included. I believe that this started the rot, and somehow tarnished Sarah and Andrew's royal image right from the start. They thought they were being fresh and original. The public saw it differently.

I bitterly regret not fighting harder with Sarah over the guest list. I fought for as long as I could, and we had some quite spectacular scenes. In the end I gave up, particularly as Sarah's mother had arrived from the Argentine to throw in her opinions as well. She came months before the wedding, anxious not to miss out on anything, so I withdrew from the fray. Arrangements for Sarah's wedding gown, and the dresses and outfits for the bridesmaids and pages were taken over by a regiment of women – Sarah, both grandmothers, plus Jane and Susie from a distance. On many occasions, Sarah wanted to tell me about the wedding dress. 'I don't want to hear a word about it,' I said. 'I just want to see it.'

One incident that was reported as a public scene between us was in fact anything but. One of the papers said that Sarah and I had a row over wedding dresses at lunch in the Causerie in Claridges, and that King Constantine had to come over to sort us out. The truth was that we were having lunch quite happily, and so was King Constantine at another table. Sarah was showing me various illustrations of hats and dresses she was considering for Ascot week that year, nothing to do with the wedding at all. Someone who observed this must have thought we were arguing, when I simply flipped one or two sketches back on to the table rather dismissively. They were awful, I admit. Simply dreadful, I might even have said.

Shortly after this, King Constantine got up from his table and came over to us. Sarah and he had met before, but this was the first time he had seen her since the engagement announcement. Someone must have thought mistakenly that he was making conciliatory gestures instead of congratulatory ones, and reported back to Fleet Street accordingly. The Claridges management was horrified, afraid that a member of their staff had tipped off the press. They didn't rest until they discovered that it had been a guest. This is just a small example of the way things were beginning to be twisted and turned inside out by the press.

If the Queen and the State were paying for the occasion, it was obviously up to me to give some sort of celebration for Sarah and Andrew in the run-up to the wedding. It took quite a time for everybody to work out just what they wanted to do, but it was more than my life was worth to be too dictatorial.

'Right, we're giving a party,' I was told by Andrew and Sarah, 'on the Tuesday of the wedding week.'

'Then I know exactly what we'll do,' I said. 'We'll give the party right on Smith's Lawn. We'll use some of the tentage already there for the International Day the following Sunday.'

Having established who was going to be invited, it was one of those pieces of organization that I really enjoy. The guest list started at 350 and soon grew to 750. I knew this would happen, bearing in mind the large number of foreign royals and heads of state who would be in the country and who must be included. Then there were Sarah's friends, Andrew's friends and anyone I wanted to invite myself. The plan was to hold a dinner for the Queen, Prince Philip and the rest of the Royal Family in advance, and then have the other guests arrive afterwards.

Now I had my own project while those around me were getting excited about theirs. I needed to choose the music, the tent-people, the caterers and the flowers. There was no mains electricity, so generators had to be provided, as did loos – really special portable ones. I asked Town and Country to do the catering. I had been dealing with them for years on the International Day, knew them all and trusted them to do a good job. They were delighted to be involved, and generously donated part of their services as a special wedding gift. The tentage was by Derek Lane and Hart & Co, and was adapted from the marquees and tents we would be using the following Sunday. Sarah made the arrangements for the band, which was organized by Major Hugh Lindsay, the Queen's Equerry, who was tragically killed in a skiing accident with the Prince of Wales's party two years later. The discotheque, run by Sarah's friend Angus Gibson, was decorated like a ship with lifebelts hung around the deck bearing the words 'HMS SARAH' or 'HMS ANDREW'. Sue was in charge of the flowers for the marquee, and friends of hers, Susie Cazenove and Daryl Cooke did them beautifully. She also arranged the seating plan, which must have been a nightmare. Members of the family were hosting tables, including Alex Makim who sat with both grandmothers. Prince and Princess Michael of Kent were due to sit at his table, but the Prince arrived without his wife.

With so many members of the Royal Family present, and other dignitaries, including Mrs Reagan, a massive security police operation was required; many meetings took place with Special Branch and the Thames Valley Police. I was determined that it should remain a private party, although there were certainly a lot of people there whom one wouldn't normally invite to a private party.

The night of the ball, all members of the media were banned from Windsor Great Park; mounted policemen patrolled the wooded areas, and frogmen scoured the lakes. Out of sight of Smith's Lawn was a massive police 'village'. The idea was to have all the necessary security without it being obvious. This was the second time I'd had a run-in with Mrs Reagan's Secret Service men. Having established that Mrs Reagan was coming to the ball, a detachment of our own Special Branch and the American Secret Service met in my office. The Special Branch officer had already spoken to me on the telephone and warned me that the head Secret Service man was likely to be rather difficult.

'Now, Major,' he began, 'tell us what this is all about.'

'It's very simple,' I told him. 'It's going to be a private party which I'm giving for my daughter before her wedding. Mrs Reagan has been invited, and has accepted. Other guests include about thirty-two members of royal families – both British and foreign – plus about five hundred others.'

'Where is the party going to be held?' the security chief asked.

'Follow me.' Off we went at a good sharp pace from my

office out to the middle of the number two ground, where I stopped.

'This is where the ball's going to be.'

The security chief looked at me in horror. 'Come on, Major, get serious, we haven't got much time. There's nothing here.'

'I know,' I replied. 'The marquee will be here, the car park there.' I tried to fire his enthusiasm by pointing around the ground to imaginary structures. I went through it all chapter and verse. The British Special Branch could hardly contain their amusement; the Americans could scarcely contain their dismay.

'What about security?' they asked. I turned to the Special Branch men, who explained how they had already met the Chief Constable of the Thames Valley Police, and that they had it all under control.

'OK,' the Americans finally conceded. 'Then we will have to have fifteen men inside the tent with Mrs Reagan.'

'No, you won't,' I said. 'The Queen will have her personal protection officer inside, and the Prince of Wales will have his. There may be one other. So Mrs Reagan will have to make do with just two of your guys.'

Later I was told that Mrs Reagan was to arrive in a heavy bullet-proof Cadillac flanked by six outriders.

'She'll get bogged down in the grass on the polo ground,' they said. 'You've got to put down a road.'

'Certainly not,' I replied.

'If she gets stuck,' they threatened, 'it will be on your head.'

I knew she wouldn't, because we had heavy horse-boxes going over the ground all the time. I wasn't worried, although I might have had the odd doubt when the English summer played true to form and sent down a few days of heavy rain just before the ball. To be on the safe side, I made sure I had the necessary ground staff and tractors on hand to pull Mrs Reagan out if she did get stuck!

The press were rushing around like ants trying to get in,

but they were frustrated by a combination of the police and the park authorities. As a result, there is no photographic record at all of the ball in progress, although we do have some pictures taken of the inside of the marquees before the guests arrived. I felt that the ball was a tremendous success, and that everyone enjoyed themselves in a relaxed way. I left at 5 a.m. happy in the knowledge that not a single thing had gone wrong. I doubt very much if a private individual has ever had to entertain quite so many royals all at once, and right in the middle of a polo ground at that!

There was one important piece of procedure that I had to get out of the way in the run-up to the wedding, and that was the question of who was going to escort Sarah's coach on the short trip from Clarence House to Westminster Abbey. When the Princess of Wales had married, she had an escort of mounted police, but I wanted them replaced with Life Guards for family reasons. My friend Johnny Johnson had now become Sir John, and Comptroller in the Lord Chamberlain's office, so my first request was to him. Whenever I wanted to know details of some aspect of the wedding arrangements, he kept me up to date.

'Sorry,' Johnny said. 'You've got to have mounted police. Or the best we could possibly do would be to give her an escort of the King's Troop, Royal Horse Artillery.'

While the King's Troop weren't exactly rivals to the Life Guards, they certainly wouldn't have been my first choice as an alternative escort. 'There's no point in having another regiment,' I said. 'We might as well have mounted police.' Undeterred, I went to see the Silver Stick of the Household Cavalry – the Colonel who was in command at that time. 'I know you have to provide an escort for the Queen's carriage,' I said. 'Could you also find enough horses and men for Sarah's carriage?'

He agreed that he could, but he had been told that an escort of mounted police had already been decided upon.

My three loyal grooms.
Above, left: John John, before the grand military gold cup, Sandown Park, on Cardinal's Drum.
Above, right: Ralph Cole at our stables at Ascot.
Below: George Smith with Cinturon (Tanky).

With Sarah aged a year,
boating on the Thames.

Jane and Sarah.
The first of many skiing
holidays.

Dear Mummy. daddy.
        Thank you very very
much   for leting us go to
Swilzland we Both enjoed
it specially sking. we loved
the teabar. and the slelta rid.
Loto of Love from
        Jane and Sarah.
        X X X X X X X
Jane X X X X Sarah.
        0 0 0 0 0 0 0
            0 0 0 0 0 0

The thank you letter.

Sarah

Jane

Sarah looking characteristically mischievous ...

... and unusually thoughtful.

Jane and Sarah on horseback.

Above, left: Guarding Daddy's cup.

Above, right: Shouldering the burden of fatherhood.

Right: Polo groupies. Sarah and Andrew as children. This is how they met, supporting their fathers on the polo field.

Determined
action.

Argentina 1966.
The English team
consisting of
(left to right)
the Marquess of
Waterford,
Patrick
Beresford,
Patrick Kemple
(Rhodesia),
Sinclair Hill
(Australia),
Paul Withers
and me.

The team led
by Rao Rajah
Hanut Singh
and his
retainers,
accompanied
by Archangel
Lord
Cowdray.
(£50 was all
you could
take out of
the country
then.)

Receiving a cup from
the Queen.

The
Royal Ousehold
versus
The Ousehold
Avalry.

Windsor Park team,
me standing in as wife
to the Prince of Wales.

Left: Polo Manager. With the Prince of Wales and Prince William.

Below: The first early morning chukkas after the Prince of Wales broke his arm. The Reptile Press lined up behind waiting for a mishap.

Bottom: The gels of the Guards Polo Club.

GUARDS POLO CLUB

'The only person who can change all this,' said Johnny Johnson, 'is the Queen.'

It just so happened that a week later there was to be a dinner party at Windsor Castle. As Andrew's prospective father-in-law I had the good fortune to be sitting next to the Queen. I took this opportunity to present my case for a Life Guards escort, explaining the background of five generations of Fergusons in the Life Guards, and I told her how much it meant to me.

'Let's look into it,' Her Majesty replied. The dinner was on a Saturday, and by Monday I was told that an escort of Life Guards could be provided.

With all the frenetic planning going on, the run-up to the wedding was one of the most tiring times of my life. When I look back on it, I wonder how we managed to cram so much in. Among the more enjoyable pre-wedding events was the cocktail party given in the Royal Mews at Buckingham Palace organized by the Crown Equerry, Sir John Miller, to show off the horses and carriages to the guests and VIPs. The afternoon before the wedding ball at Smith's Lawn, I was playing polo on an adjacent ground – and I had played the day previously, too. The fortnight prior to the wedding also featured the Dummer christening for Jane's daughter, Ayesha, and a village garden party was held at Dummer the weekend before. It was all quite exhausting. We could never have managed without the help of Annie Foster-Firth who came to Dummer specifically to mastermind everything at home for the wedding time. She was incredible, with boundless energy and enthusiasm – a godsend.

Because I am, generally speaking, a non-drinker, I always drive back when we've been to London for a function. If I go to a party, the maximum I ever drink is two or three glasses of wine. I've always hated brandy and port, and it must be thirty years since I've touched gin or whisky. What is the use of being a sportsman if you're a heavy drinker? One night shortly before the wedding, I was driving home with Sue at around two a.m. and I knew I was very tired. To counteract the sleepiness and stay alert on the motorway, first I opened the car window. Then I removed my jacket. The idea was to get cold enough to stay awake, but it was midsummer so by the time we reached Dummer, I had no shirt on and no socks and shoes either, and I'd puffed away on far too many cigarettes. I needed to keep my energy levels somehow so I asked a few people what they recommended. Sue's sister Diana put us on to Regina royal jelly, and I found it helped enormously. I have taken two tablets every morning ever since, and recommended it to Sarah, too. It gives that extra boost.

I had little to do with the actual wedding preparations. An army of women was sorting out the bridesmaids' dresses and pages' uniforms. Alice, Andrew and Seamus were all to be part of the wedding party, as bridesmaid and pageboys, so excitement was mounting at Dummer. My own wedding outfit was never in dispute. I would be wearing my father's morning coat, made for him in 1921, which had stood me in good stead over many years. I'd worn it to my own two weddings, as well as Jane's. Its wonderful original material has taken on a slightly green tinge over the years, but it is regularly updated, retrimmed with new braid, and the lining replaced. If someone had told me to get a new morning coat, I wouldn't have taken the slightest bit of notice. I did have a piece of extra fabric put into the back of the waistcoat, which was inexplicably tighter since I'd worn it last, and I bought a new pair of black shoes, but only because I needed them. I wore an ordinary white shirt, nothing special or new, but I did have a special haircut by Mr Conway at Trumpers in Curzon Street, where I have been going for nearly fifty years. I've used Mr Trumper's Essence of Limes ever since I first discovered aftershave, and I certainly wore it on the wedding day, although the effects had probably worn off by the time we reached the Abbey.

I was furious when I discovered I was not to be allowed to sit next to Sue in the front pew. It wasn't that I minded sitting next to Susie; I wanted to be allowed to sit next to my wife. Etiquette demanded otherwise, however, and after a few heated discussions, I had to back down. Even the Queen couldn't help me here.

The night before the wedding, the Ferguson family moved into the Belgravia Sheraton in Pont Street, Knightsbridge, admirably managed then by Doreen Boulding. They did a wonderful job of accommodating us all, and it was ideally located for the next day's activities. I fell asleep over the main course at dinner. Sue still laughs about it. How could I ever qualify as a womanizer, she says, when I can fall asleep while surrounded by beautiful women?

Later that night, I found my second wind and set out with Jane to drive down the Mall and see what was happening. I couldn't believe that all the crowds assembling on either side of the wedding route had come to see my daughter. I was keen to visit the Dummer contingent. They were camping out overnight, at the end of the Mall, equipped with their 'WE ARE FROM DUMMER' sign, and included the daughters of our neighbours, Charles and Patti Palmer Tomkinson. The atmosphere was electric, almost tangible.

That night before the wedding, as was the tradition, Sarah stayed with the Queen Mother. Earlier that evening, she couldn't resist slipping out from Clarence House into the crowd, dressed casually in sweater and jeans. It wasn't long before a cry of recognition went up, but not before she had been able to experience for herself some of that unique atmosphere. I was able to have a quick chat with her on the telephone before we all retired for the night, and she was in good spirits, very excited about what was to come.

I couldn't find my braces the following morning. They hadn't made it up to London from Dummer. Taking the chance of accompanying Sarah up the aisle without them was unthinkable, so, after a moment of panic, someone from the hotel very kindly rushed out and bought some from Harrods. We then set off to Clarence House where there was masses of hanging around, something I'm not terribly good at. There was nothing to do but drink coffee and eat biscuits while everyone around me was freaking out. Sue rushed upstairs to help get the children ready, and there was another drama when it was discovered that the pageboys' collars were too tight. Andrew and Seamus Makim were the worst affected, but Sue managed to get the man from Gieves & Hawkes, the tailors who had made the miniature midshipman's uniforms, to loosen them sufficiently for comfort.

My great friend Alistair Aird (now Sir Alistair), whom I had known since Eton and Sandhurst days, was the Queen Mother's Assistant Private Secretary, so I spent some of the time chatting to him. Then I had a stroll outside to talk to the Life Guards escort who were waiting to accompany us to the Abbey. I already knew one or two of them, so this helped while away the time. I felt churned up and excited because so many of my family were involved, not only Sarah. I was anxious for everything to go right, but the proceedings were not in my hands and I felt frustrated at not being able to do more than what I was told, put on my old coat and get on with it – or not get on with it, as it seemed that morning.

I remember deciding I had to stop drinking coffee. I didn't want to be in the embarrassing situation of needing to pee. No one would be able to go to the loo for hours; we'd all have to wait until we got back to Buckingham Palace. The television was on in Clarence House, so you could see what was happening, watch people arriving at the Abbey, hear the cheers. I wasn't feeling at all nervous or apprehensive; I was more nervous as to how I was going to treat Sarah, what I was going to do to keep her relaxed on the way down to the Abbey in the carriage. I need not have worried. She appeared at the top of the stairs in that beautiful dress, looking absolutely stunning, and uttered those memorable words, 'Who the hell is standing on my train?' Fortunately, the rest of the party had departed by then, and didn't hear her.

My top hat did not accompany us to Westminster Abbey. The media reported afterwards that I had left it behind at the Sheraton, but the truth is that I never intended to wear it anyway. I felt sorry for the poor naval officer whose job it was to look after my hat. His entire role in the wedding ceremony was redundant.

The walk up the aisle seemed to take ages, though officially it was four minutes. On the way Sarah was so relaxed she was cracking jokes with me, making comments about the guests and their outfits. When we reached the archway leading to the chancel, with the Queen and Prince Andrew gazing down expectantly, I had to say, 'Come on. You've got to be serious now.'

When the ceremony was over, I joined the Queen in her open-topped landau for the ride back down the Mall to Buckingham Palace. For me, this was quite an ironic moment. Once, I reflected, I had been part of the Sovereign's Escort of Life Guards who rode alongside this coach – now here I was riding inside it. I remember looking round to the Commander of the Escort, Seymour Gilbert Denham, who had been one of my subalterns in Cyprus. With him was David Waterhouse, another officer. As I got in, they were saluting the Queen. I gave them a huge wink and a grin because I had done their job so often myself.

The first time I had been in their boots was for a State Opening of Parliament, and I had to be on the right-hand wheel of the royal coach. I had discussed the procedure with my father, who had done it himself in his day. 'You have to have your left boot right alongside the right wheel hub,' he had explained. 'The Queen sits on the right-hand side, so if your boot is there, you're very close in case anything happens.'

But rules and regulations change over the years, and now it

was your horse's head that needed to be alongside the wheel hub, not your boot. The way I was riding, the crowd couldn't see anything. When we got to the Houses of Parliament, before alighting from the carriage, the Queen leaned forward to speak to me. My heart leaped. I thought she was going to say, 'Well done, that was a very good escort.' What she said was, 'Ronald, please remember in future, they've come to see me and not you.'

Now, the crowds had come to see us both.

Poor Sue. I had quite a pang of sympathy for her, but there was nothing I could do. There was I, riding back to Buckingham Palace with the Queen. Right behind us, my former wife was travelling in a carriage with Prince Philip. Two of our children and our grandson were also part of this procession, and they rode in another coach with Linda, their nanny. Sue, who had been made to sit behind me throughout the wedding service, then had to journey back to Buckingham Palace alone.

All I remember saying to the Queen on the way back was, 'How fantastic, look at all this.' You could scarcely make yourself heard because of the noise. Half-way up the Mall, I spotted the Dummer contingent and pointed them out to the Queen, who gave them a special wave. Our carriage arrived first at the Palace, and the Queen nipped off smartly to freshen up. Then all the photographs had to be taken before lunch. The children really enjoyed it – I was so proud of them, they behaved immaculately even though Alice and Seamus were only five, and Andrew seven.

By the time we had got back for the wedding breakfast, everything was working like clockwork, but I still felt strange to be part of a pageant that somebody else had organized. The whole thing seemed unreal, like a trance. I went with the flow, as my children would say. We all stepped out onto the balcony, filled from one end to the other with pages, bridesmaids, royals, fathers, mothers and aunts. Sue almost had to be forced onto it. She was cropped out of many of the official photographs when they were published because she was standing right at the end. I couldn't believe her bad luck. She had contributed so much time, effort and help to the wedding, particularly with regard to the children.

One hundred and forty of us sat down to the wedding breakfast, a cold buffet of lobster and lamb cutlets, followed by strawberries and cream. There was an epic cake, a 240-pounder baked by chefs from the Royal Navy supply school at Torpoint in Cornwall, and Sarah and Andrew cut it with a ceremonial sword. Unlike an ordinary wedding, there had been no receiving line on the way in, and there were no speeches, either. The Queen was happy, everyone was happy – it really was a jolly, relaxed family occasion.

When the time came for the bride and bridegroom to depart, we all went down to the courtyard and inspected their carriage, which had been decorated by Prince Edward and bore a large teddy bear and a silver satellite dish with the message: 'Phone Home'. As Sarah and Andrew came down the stairs, and prepared to depart, it was an extraordinarily emotional moment for me. The others went for the confetti and rose petals, and I grabbed my son, Andrew, by the hand, and walked off out of the gates of the Palace. I just wanted to get away from everybody, much to their consternation. 'Where the hell is he going now?' I heard someone murmur. It must have seemed rather unusual, with the Queen standing there, for one of the party to walk out, but for me this was the final moment at the end of a highly emotional day. We stood just outside the gates, and as Sarah and Andrew's carriage swept left round the Queen Victoria statue in front of the palace and turned right for Chelsea Hospital, I said my private goodbyes, and finally let go of my daughter.

At Chelsea Hospital, they were picked up by helicopter, the first leg of their journey, and taken to join the Royal Yacht *Britannia* for a honeymoon cruise around the Azores. That evening, there was to be a VIP-studded ball at Claridges, organized by Lady Elizabeth Anson, the Queen's cousin, and attended by all the visiting heads of state and royalty. It was a really smart occasion, yet as soon as I had heard about it, I had decided not to go. My family thought I was crazy. How could I turn down something like this, when everyone else would be there? Sue was particularly surprised. I was adamant. My place was at Dummer. I wanted to be with the people I had lived with since I was a child. The villagers had been celebrating all day, and that evening they were having a special barbecue, and I wanted to be there. The farm staff had returned from their own wonderful day – they had been taken to London by special bus, and had lunch at the Savoy. For my part, I'd had enough pomp and circumstance, and I drove the children and nannies home, leaving the rest of the family to enjoy Claridges.

Once home, I quickly changed back into casual clothes and took the dogs for a short walk around the fields. As I did this, Sarah rang me, from somewhere on her journey, and I was terribly upset to have missed her call. The message was, she would try and ring back, which she did, much later that night.

There was no doubt in my mind that I made the right decision to leave London when I did. The village people had been subjected to an awful lot of unnecessary hassle over the preceding months, and the press had given them a hard time; the very least I could do was to be there. The children were all exhausted and were soon put to bed by their nanny, but I stayed to watch the fireworks and to reflect on the amazing ceremonial spectacular in which I had just played my most memorable supporting role.

CHAPTER FIFTEEN

Cracks and Criticisms

THE SUNDAY after Sarah's wedding was that all important last Sunday in July, the International Polo Day at Smith's Lawn, sponsored by Cartier. This year, there would be even more VIPs attending than ever – many had stayed on in London after the wedding. The crowd would top twenty-five thousand, and as the International's Director I had a much more active role than the one I had played as father of the bride. For that, all the organizational work and attention to detail had been done for me. For the International, it was my responsibility to make sure everything worked.

I left Dummer Down House very early on that Sunday morning and shot up the motorway at a cracking pace. A police car appeared from nowhere and flagged me down.

'Where are you going in such a hurry on a Sunday morning?' the officer asked.

I started to explain, as he peered into my car more closely. 'Oh – it's Major Ferguson!' he exclaimed. 'You had a terrific day on Thursday. Great wedding. It was a wonderful occasion, sir. Off you go – and be careful.'

Instant recognition like this happened to me a lot over the months immediately after the wedding. I was always pleased to talk to people about Sarah. It was a thrill – as it would be for any father – to have a cab driver turn round when you're in his cab and congratulate you on having such a lovely daughter. Some people misinterpreted my actions and thought that I was courting publicity for myself, which was ludicrous. I was very proud of my daughter, and I loved to hear her being complimented, but it was she they wanted to know about, not me.

With hindsight, I probably did make myself too available to the press, and because I appeared to be so accessible, they thought I had given them permission to be over-familiar. People didn't understand that I was a private individual answering my own telephone. I had no help whatsoever from the Buckingham Palace press office. They had made it clear from the beginning that, although I was the bride's father, there would be no support or cover from them.

After the wedding, things calmed down and we could almost pick up our normal lives. I had to get used to the fact that my daughter was now a duchess – the Queen had conferred the title of Duke of York on Prince Andrew at 8 a.m. on the morning of the wedding. Sarah had to adjust to living in the somewhat cramped quarters of Andrew's bachelor apartment at Buckingham Palace, and to resign herself to the knowledge that she might have married a prince, but she had also married a serving naval officer who would spend long periods away from home. Those early days must have been tough for Sarah. Her office had been moved into the Palace. For a girl used to freedom and independence, she now no longer went out to work neither was she ever off duty. Instead, she had to learn how to fit in with the established Palace traditions and protocol.

Buckingham Palace is enormous, but there is very little living accommodation or privacy. Sarah's first married home consisted of a double bedroom and bathroom, a sitting room with a conference table and office in it, another bedroom which was used as an office, and another bathroom. There was no front door; the rooms weren't self-contained, so people were coming in and out all the time. The rooms led out directly on to the corridor, with the Princess Royal's offices just a few doors down. They were so short of space that all Sarah's clothes had to be kept in wardrobes in the corridor, and many of their wedding presents were stacked there too.

Although a degree of formality obviously had to be observed in public, Sarah's life with her own family scarcely changed. The only difference was that whenever she came down to Dummer, which she did frequently when Andrew was away, she would be accompanied by her detective, and we had to have extra security arrangements here. The papers printed a good deal of rubbish about her getting grand. She may have been grand in front of her staff, or in the car coming down here – but when she arrived, she reverted to being Sarah, wearing a pair of jeans and being told to wash up and clear away the dishes. Why not? It was what she had always done, and we weren't going to change our attitudes towards her.

Prince Andrew wasn't grand either. When he arrived here to spend a day or a weekend, he couldn't have been easier and nicer. He was at his happiest being left alone in front of the television set. I didn't feel I had to sit and entertain him or talk to him, we just carried on as normal. Andrew was marvellous with the children, and got on particularly well with my son Andrew. On one occasion when I was unable to attend a fathers v. sons golf match at Andrew's school, Prince Andrew stood in for me. They did badly – both of them had only just started to play – but that didn't matter. Andrew was extremely relaxed and easy to get along with. I know there have been reports of him being rude and arrogant, but he was never rude to me or Sue. If there were just four of us we would sit around the kitchen table for dinner. We weren't going to go into the dining room and light candles and change into evening clothes just because he was with us.

Undoubtedly it was Sarah's naturalness that had first endeared her to the Royal Family, if not to some of its stuffier members. Joining that family is much harder than anyone realizes. It is a rather staid household, with plenty of bowing and scraping from servants and courtiers. Yet Sarah has always liked to get things going, so she used to make the Queen sit down and play card games, which the Queen loves. At the wedding reception, my mother said to the Queen, 'You're very kind to Sarah.'

'She's so nice to us,' the Queen replied. 'Sarah cheats even more than my mother at Racing Demon.'

'I taught Sarah how to play,' said my mother.

The Queen laughed. 'Then you must be the cause!'

Sadly, it didn't take long for the gilt on the media ginger-bread to wear off. From being hailed as the new star, the breath of fresh air, she was soon criticized about the way she dressed, the way she walked, the amount of time she spent out of the country. She was compared unfavourably with the Princess of Wales, which is grossly unfair. They are totally different shapes in build. Some of the clothes she wore were awful, but she would not be told. It wasn't my place to tell her what to wear, but many of the people who did advise her were wrong.

The Princess of Wales had a St Michael's Mount of Duchy of Cornwall money to spend on clothes, which Sarah did not. People thought that marrying into the Royal Family meant you never had to think about money again – they were completely wrong. Andrew has little money of his own. He has his naval pay, and an allowance from the Civil List, and Sarah had her own small trust fund, but out of this they had to pay for many of their own staff and household expenses. Sarah could not just go off and spend money whenever she wanted to.

To a certain extent, becoming the Duchess of York did go to her head. She didn't always read the rule book properly. In the Royal Family certain privileges are there for the taking, but there have to be limits. Sarah thought she could get away with much more than she did. In those early days Andrew should have been strong enough to guide her and advise her, but he didn't.

The number of holidays and foreign assignments she undertook brought adverse comments, and she was dubbed 'Freebie Fergie' by the press. She did have a lot of holidays. When Andrew was away at sea, she was bored, and had a lot of time on her hands. Her trips abroad weren't all holidays though the press made out that they were, such as the two occasions when she went to present prizes at the Combined Services Ski Association and took some days to go skiing herself.

What is the definition of a freebie? Whenever Sarah travelled privately, she paid for her own airline tickets, although those tickets were probably upgraded. Air travel is a competitive business – airlines will bend over backwards to upgrade VIPs to first class if they think they will get good publicity. Journalists get offered freebies too – free travel, free samples, free food and drink. On the polo ground, journalists often expected hospitality and refreshments. I would suggest that next time they should bring their own sandwiches!

It struck me as grossly hypocritical when some newspapers implied that Sarah was asking designers to donate clothes to her, when half their fashion editors were walking around in free outfits. Do you suppose that the Princess of Wales pays for all her own clothes, or that the designers always remember to send the invoice? Look what Diana has already done for Benetton and Thorpe Park, for McDonald's and Planet Hollywood. No doubt Euro-Disney had a few more people through its gates as a result of Sarah taking her children there. Where do you draw the line? What is the difference between a member of the Royal Family accepting hospitality, or attending a charity ball, knowing a lot of tickets will be sold because of their presence?

One of the most recent pieces of blatant hypocrisy was the sneering that went on in the summer of 1993 when Sarah was seen driving a new XJ Jaguar. It was a car loaned to Andrew to try; he then loaned it to Sarah. Jaguar must have been thrilled with the publicity, as Mercedes had been when Diana drove one. What people don't realize is that a massive number of Ford cars within the royal fleet are also on semi-permanent loan from Ford. A large number of newspaper motoring correspondents enjoy the same privileges, with even smarter cars, but that isn't written about.

Another problem for Sarah was being compared all the time with the Princess Royal in the number of official engagements they were each carrying out. Sarah's list of public engagements was, in fact, daunting. The press never reported the behind-the-scenes work that went on. She might invite one of the sick children she had met on a hospital visit back to Buckingham Palace for tea, or a teddy bear would be sent out with a personal message from her. Sarah is incredibly thoughtful towards other people and always has been.

Nineteen eighty-eight was a pretty grim year, one way and another, despite the birth of the lovely, lively Beatrice. In March there was the skiing tragedy in Klosters when Major Hugh Lindsay was killed in an avalanche and our good friend and neighbour, Patti Palmer Tomkinson, was badly injured. The 'scandal' of the Wigmore Club broke in April, and Jane's marriage, which had been unhappy for some time, finally broke up amid a glare of publicity both here and in Australia, which was particularly upsetting as she was so far away. Then in the autumn of that year I was not re-elected to my position at the Guards Polo Club.

Criticism of Sarah continued almost unabated. Some of the worst came after the birth of Beatrice, who arrived on 8 August. Sarah had put on a lot of weight during her pregnancy, and Fleet Street's Killer Bimbos were out in force to get her. When she let it be known that she would be leaving her baby to fly to Australia to see her husband and spend some time with her sister, they moved in for the kill. An enormous amount of rubbish was printed in the women's pages about 'bonding' and Sarah was branded a poor mother. Prior to this the press had taken another sideways swipe at her when they made a song and dance about me – my charity appearance on the Dame Edna Everage show dressed as a punk, and my membership of the Wigmore Club didn't help Sarah's image. It did seem that, having long castigated the Royal Family for being aloof, removed from reality and dull in appearance and attitudes, the media felt uncomfortable with anything else, and moved swiftly to crush any signs of life and originality. An outcry went up when Sarah and Princes Andrew and Edward appeared in the *It's A Royal Knockout* television show – but this was a fund-raising charity event. Eyebrows were also raised when Sarah was seen horsing around on the ski slopes with Diana, or playing the fool with an umbrella at Ascot. Her natural high spirits – the very qualities that had endeared her to the media in the first place – were frowned upon. Now, with her so-called abandonment of baby Beatrice, they thought they had hit the jackpot.

I had been instrumental in advising her to leave the baby behind. Having been on two or three royal tours myself, I knew it was crazy to drag a tiny baby along. Beatrice was of an age when she was perfectly happy staying behind with her excellent nanny, and it was in her interest, as opposed to media and public interest, for her to remain at Castlewood House, the property near Ascot that had been lent to Sarah and Andrew by King Hussein of Jordan while their own house was being built.

Sunninghill Park, the Queen's wedding present to them both, created more ammunition for the press. They dubbed it 'South York' – a pun on the name of the house in the popular *Dallas* television series – and seemed determined to use it to project the image they had already invented for the young royal couple. Andrew and Sarah were portrayed as tasteless *nouveaux riches* hedonists who mixed only with pop stars and other showbiz celebrities. This was quite unjustified: Sarah had worked hard in the early days to help Andrew improve his image. His clothes, when they married, were diabolical. Like all the male members of the Royal Family, he had tended to adopt the Teutonic style of dress favoured by Prince Philip. Diana had to revamp the Prince of Wales's wardrobe, and Sarah certainly needed to use her influence over Andrew's.

Sunninghill Park was a practical, easy-to-run establishment, which it needed to be for security reasons, with a good walled garden and well-shaped rooms. I had been shown the plans but I had little to do with the discussions that revolved around it. I liked it very much, particularly as it was just a short stroll from my offices – I was by then working for the Royal County of Berkshire Polo Club. Even when Sarah wasn't at home, it meant I could go and sit on her verandah with a cup of coffee and relax.

Eugenie was born on 23 March 1990, a much less placid baby than Beatrice had been, but with beautiful blue eyes and dark red hair. I felt, rather than knew, that all was not well between Sarah and Andrew, but it has never been my style to pry. When they had first married, she had been trying to do her job and he his job, and things wouldn't have gone wrong if he had been around more. It doesn't matter who you are, you need your husband there when you're pregnant. Andrew had flown back only at the last minute to be with her before Beatrice's birth, and this rankled. When he did come home on leave, it was difficult for Sarah to accept some of his behaviour. She would have been longing to see him for weeks yet, as I've said, he liked nothing better than to be left alone in front of the television screen watching a video or a film. This was his idea of relaxation, but it drove Sarah wild.

When they invited friends round for dinner, I witnessed first hand how Andrew would serve himself first and start eating, oblivious to his guests' needs. Coming from a family that put hospitality and good manners high on the priority list, Sarah found this hard to take. She had been brought up in a household where it was traditional for the man to do the carving, yet at her dinner parties she did the carving herself. Being the stronger character, I suppose she thought she would just get on with it. As a traditionalist I would have liked to have seen Andrew do it, and if he didn't know how, his staff could surely have shown him.

Andrew is physically tough, but mentally he is not. I never thought of him as pompous, although I know others who did. Even though at times he could be thoughtless, I always respected him enormously, but he should have been tougher with Sarah. She had more than once sought his support when she had become embroiled in a disagreement with the Palace establishment: she continued to find it hard to win the respect of the inner circle of courtiers at the Palace who live in fear of change – and their jobs. No help was forthcoming from Andrew in that department. There was speculation in the press that he bullied Sarah into behaving the way he wanted her to but, given their personalities, nothing could be further from the truth. Andrew's macho image belies a much milder-mannered personality than you would expect.

When things started to go wrong between them, I know that Andrew even broached the subject of leaving the navy, but Sarah wouldn't hear of it. She didn't want a disgruntled civilian on her conscience, so she was forced to carry on alone, in the face of what seemed like never-ending criticism. She was still determined to be natural, but ought to have looked at herself more closely. She got carried away with her 'what you see is what you get' attitude, and the walls began to close in. Her next moves, in trying to break free of what she saw as impossible restraints, were to prove disastrous.

CHAPTER SIXTEEN

The Reptile Pen

MY FIRST ENCOUNTERS with the press occurred long before there was any hint of a romance between Sarah and Prince Andrew. I had been dealing with them for many years, and for the most part my relationship with them had been nothing but cordial. As Deputy Chairman of the Guards Polo Club, it was part of my job to look after press enquiries; I had to make sure the press were in the right area to obtain their photographs, and I was on hand to answer their queries. If the Buckingham Palace press office received any questions about polo and the Prince of Wales, they would refer them to me; they know nothing about the game, so they couldn't give a first-hand or accurate account. More often than not, the only queries were as to how the Prince of Wales was feeling after he had fallen off!

The Prince of Wales attracted a lot of attention on the polo ground from the moment he started playing in 1970, and press interest certainly built up in the early years before his marriage, when he would turn up with various girlfriends. In those days, we allowed reporters and cameramen to stand wherever they wanted within the members' enclosure. The Prince of Wales's engagement and subsequent marriage made him even more newsworthy. Reporters and cameramen turned up in their droves, hoping for informal shots of him with Diana. This coincided with a time when the Guards Polo Club had gained many new members, so we had to put all the press on the other side of the ground, where they could take photographs but not make life uncomfortable for anyone else. When the Prince of Wales played at other clubs, the same rules were applied.

There are strict rules for taking photographs in royal parks, and as the Guards Polo Club ground is in Windsor Great Park, members of the press needed official press passes and car parking permits before they were allowed in. This also meant that we had the right to remove their passes if any of them misbehaved. Over the years, I think only one or two were taken away, usually for disobeying instructions or inconveniencing members. Newspapers such as the *Daily Telegraph* and *The Times* and 'country' magazines – *The Field, Country Life* and *Horse and Hound* – were the only publications who took it seriously; the rest were there to take sensational photographs for the tabloids.

Eventually, as press interest increased, I decided to put all reporters in something we referred to as the Reptile Pen. Not surprisingly, they objected.

'Right,' said their spokesman. 'If you're going to do that,' they told me, 'we'll put our cameras down when the cup is presented.'

They did just that, stood in front of the Prince of Wales with their arms folded.

'You can put your cameras down for as long as you like,' I said. 'It doesn't worry me.'

Neither did it worry the sponsors, who have their own photographer anyway. They never published any polo photographs unless the Prince of Wales had fallen off, so I couldn't have cared less. I received several letters from newspaper editors, but we stuck to our guns. From then on, they had the Reptile Pen, and they knew perfectly well that they only had to step out of line once and their permits would be taken away. I appointed one of my staff as 'Reptile Keeper' to make sure they behaved. He was a 6 foot 4 ex-paratrooper with a big presence. As with all my staff, he was strictly forbidden to use physical force. Fortunately, he never had to.

Arthur Edwards of the *Sun*, who's a tremendous supporter of Sarah, became their senior spokesman and I used to rely on him to see that they all behaved.

Looking back, we had few problems once the ground rules had been established. On a personal front, once the romance between Sarah and Andrew became public knowledge, the situation changed. To give an example, there was one day when Sarah was at Dummer, at a time when she was being followed everywhere by the press. They wanted to write about how Sarah and Andrew had met, and their romance. Sarah had come by car and wanted to leave without anybody knowing where she was going. The press was firmly installed at the bottom of the drive, with several motor cycles and cars, all revved up and waiting to follow the minute her car appeared.

However, what they hadn't taken into account was how well we know the local area, and that some of our neighbours' drives have more than one exit. So, with my farm foreman, we made a plan. I drove Sarah's car down the drive, with Sarah visible in the passenger seat, and turned right at the bottom. The farm foreman was in a Land-rover behind us, and behind the Land-rover, another farm worker followed in a tractor and trailer. No one could get past. One motor cyclist thought he was being frightfully clever and tried to overtake on the road, but the tractor driver was quite smart and he ended up in the hedge. Fortunately, he wasn't hurt. When we got to our neighbour's front gate, we went through, but the foreman stopped the Land-rover right in the gate, so no one could follow. Sarah and I detoured round our neighbour's house, and out the other side, where I got out of the car. She then drove off on a route the press would never have dreamed existed, and it meant she could disappear off down the motorway. I met all the reporters back in the village, rushing around like ants trying to find out where she had gone. They begged me to tell them, but I just shrugged my shoulders and walked on home.

On another occasion, Sarah was having her hair done in London, and needed to leave to meet Prince Andrew, but she had discovered that the press had staked out the car park where she had left her car. Fortunately I happened to be in London, so she rang me, explained what was happening, and asked if she could use my car. I drove up to the hairdresser's in Albemarle Street, left my car outside, collected her parking ticket, and then strolled up to the Burlington Garage in Piccadilly, where all the reporters were waiting. You should have seen their disconsolate faces when I arrived to drive Sarah's car away. 'Where is she? Where is she?' they cried.

They were games, but they were important games to her and I didn't mind playing them because it was one up on the prying journalists.

My relationship with the press certainly changed when Sarah's engagement was announced. As I said earlier, it was the day I was due to fly to Australia to judge and umpire the spring show of the Australian Polo Association. The day before I left, I had a call from the Palace press office, with whom I had previously only ever discussed polo matters. They advised me to say nothing when I reached Australia, except that I was very happy. I thought that was the most absurd advice and I told them so.

I flew to Australia by Air Canada. When I got on the flight, I discovered a reporter from the *News of the World* sitting three rows behind me. An hour or so into the flight, a bottle of brandy arrived from the reporter. I thought, Do I accept this, or do I send it back? I don't drink brandy, but I thought it would make a good present. So after a bit I got up and stretched my legs. As I was wandering down the aisle, the reporter came up to me. I thanked her for the brandy, and told her I would give it to my son-in-law.

She said, 'I've been told to get a story from you and to follow you in Australia until I do.'

I suggested she got off at Singapore and went home. 'You won't get a story from me now or ever,' I told her. They never did get a story from me, but they dredged up several alleged to be about me in the future!

As far as I was concerned, I had a job of work to do paid for by the Sydney Easter Horse Show. I suspected that when I arrived in Sydney, I wouldn't be met by just one reporter, but by a crowd. I was right. When we landed, I was greeted by the airport manager who said, 'There are about seventy cameras and reporters out there, so we've put them all into one room, with the agreement of your daughter Jane. The press say that if you'll sit down and speak with them now, they'll leave you alone for the rest of the trip.'

So there they were, all in one big room. I sat on a sofa with Jane on one side and my son-in-law Alex Makim on the other. I thanked them for coming, told them why I was in Sydney, and explained that after this press conference, I didn't want to be bothered or telephoned. It took about forty-five minutes, while they asked relatively simple questions, such as when the wedding would take place. (I hadn't a clue – I didn't know this until four days later, when Sarah rang and told me.)

They were as good as their word. After that, I didn't see the press, or have a single telephone call from them throughout my Australian trip, whereas if I had followed the Buckingham Palace press office advice, the three weeks probably would have been very difficult.

My real problems with the press didn't start until much later. It was interesting that when there was trouble, it wasn't the well-known royal reporters and photographers or the ones that I had known from the polo ground who hounded me. It was the paparazzi, who are of a different calibre. They soon became remarkably tedious, camped semi-permanently at the bottom of my drive, waiting minute by minute for the smallest thing to happen.

My views on this are strong, and I understand that journalists have to do what they're told to do by their editors, but I still feel their behaviour is a gross intrusion of privacy. They hung about taking silly photographs of me driving in and out. They tried to talk to the farm staff, or the people in Dummer, desperately looking for a story. On many occasions Sue was followed as she drove the children to school, and quite rightly she got extremely angry. The farm staff have now become expert at not allowing journalists up the drive. My mother, who lives nearby, is an excellent mimic and if anyone rings her doorbell looking for Lady Elmhirst, she puts on an Irish or Cockney accent and pretends to be the daily. When something went wrong – in my, Sarah's or Jane's lives – it wasn't uncommon to find fifteen to twenty cars at the bottom of the drive; in the end, the local police decided they were a traffic hazard. They had to park a distance away and stand in the rain.

One morning at 5.30 a.m. there was a loud knock on the front door. This set off our three Jack Russells in a frenzy of barking. I went to the bedroom window and put my head out. I saw six people outside the front door, three reporters and three photographers.

'Yes?' I said.

'We're from the press, we'd like you to come down now to speak to us and be photographed.' At 5.30 a.m.!

I used a strong expletive, and put the window down.

The following day one of the tabloids reported, 'The Major put his head out of the window wearing his blue striped jim-jams' (which I don't wear) 'and had no comment to make.' Great! They couldn't even get the quote right.

Sometimes they would come to the front door late at night, and there were persistent late telephone calls. I didn't want to switch the telephone off or put on the answering machine, because I have responsibilities to my family, and to Jane in Australia. I might get calls from the press up to 2 a.m., saying, 'Have you seen tomorrow's paper?'

To which I'd reply, 'As it's now past midnight and I'm down in the country, how could I have?'

In some ways, they were a useful intelligence system. I would know what was going to be in a tabloid the following day because a rival paper would ring up, tell me, then ask me to comment. Now the reporters have learned that it is a complete waste of time trying to contact me: I won't speak to them under any circumstances, whether they telephone or knock on the door. I just become progressively ruder. What a terrible waste of time and money it is to have a photographer sitting at the bottom of my drive all day on a Sunday expecting Sarah to turn up. Once, a local gamekeeper found a photographer half-way up a tree, in our neighbour's woods half a mile away, complete with a long-lensed camera. The gamekeeper simply took the ladder away . . .

To give an example of how things can go wrong, I was doing an interview before the wedding with John Osmond of BBC Radio 4 – I knew him quite well as we had been in Cyprus together. John asked me the name of Sarah's first pony and I said it was a horrible little Shetland called Nigger. Then the next thing we knew, someone from the reptile press rang and said that the Committee for Racial Equality were going to sue us and what was I going to do about that. What was I going to do about what? I asked.

'Using that word,' they said. 'Are you going to apologize?'

'Apologize for what?' I said.

'Using that word on the radio.'

'I was asked a question about the pony's name. That's all.'

The Press thought this was hilarious.

It was a very sad day in April 1991 when we made the decision to dispose of the Dumanor herd of Friesians which my father started in 1948. As a result of the sale, three long-time employees had to be made redundant and although they had six months' notice and excellent terms it was a time of low morale on the farm. Fortunately two of the men almost immediately obtained positions on another farm. Contrary to press reports, nobody was sacked and no one was evicted from their cottage. In fact one person not only received the generous redundancy terms, he was also allowed to live in his cottage rent free for twelve months.

One reporter came to the door trying to make a big story out of it. As I explained to him my reasons for getting rid of the herd, I looked down and noticed that my little rough-haired Jack Russell Biggles was quietly cocking his leg all over the reporter's trousers. I could hardly keep a straight face.

The farm is now solely arable under the control of the loyal Michael Borlase assisted by Andrew Crane who between them produce superb harvests.

On several occasions the newspapers seem deliberately to have misrepresented me. We had a piece of land the other side of Dummer village which wasn't particularly good, so we put it up for sale, again for reasons of farming policy. The press got frightfully excited about that and thought we must be selling everything. We sold some land at the top of the village – now part of the golf course – so we could concentrate on having all the land in one place. It was a good commercial deal, but the papers would have you believe it was because I was broke.

Now I reached the stage where there is no point in taking up anything that's incorrect; it is better just to shrug your shoulders and let them get on with it. As someone said, most aptly, today's newspaper is tomorrow's fish and chip paper. If you are in the public eye, they are going to try to get stories and take photographs, and there's nothing you can do about it. But true professionals, like Ross Benson of the *Daily Express*, Nigel Dempster of the *Daily Mail* or Bob Graham who used to be with *Today*, have never done me any harm. They have always telephoned in advance to check out a story. If anything ever got into their columns that was inaccurate or untrue, they always printed a correction. Bob Graham has even acted as a benevolent 'mole', letting me know what is going on behind the scenes and what is likely to appear next.

One reporter who has tried to befriend me is James Whitaker of the *Daily Mirror*. He never makes any bones that his interest is journalistic; if there is a story to be told about me or Sarah or any member of my family, he'll write it. But Whitaker, like Bob Graham, has tipped me the wink about a story that's about to appear. Normally I can't do anything about it, but at least I've been forewarned. Sometimes he has called me and asked for 'guidance'. I've learned to distrust the word but on many occasions he has needed it when he was about to print something totally untrue.

I did take legal action against a newspaper once. I sued the *Sunday People* in 1990. I was in America publicizing the *Pimm's Book of Polo*, which I had edited. I went on the *Arsenio Hall Show* to promote it, a well-known chat show produced in Los Angeles. A few days later the *Sunday People* headline said 'FERGIE'S DAD IN CHAT SHOW RUMPUS.' Apparently I had been drunk on the show, and had a row with Arsenio at the party afterwards. In fact, the show was recorded at 4.30 p.m. I was only there for twenty minutes before we went on. Immediately afterwards I had had to rush off to do something else, and there was no party. It was a total fabrication. The *Sunday People* sent out two reporters to investigate; they couldn't believe how it had come about. The reporter was sacked, and they paid damages out of court.

The morning after my granddaughter Beatrice's christening, the *Sun* said that Sue had been banned from the ceremony, while on the same page there was a photograph of her *at* the christening! I rang the editor, pointed out what the problem was, and said I wanted a donation for my wife's favourite charity – which at the time was Birthright – of not less than £5000, plus an apology. They complied unquestioningly.

The press has certainly tried to crucify me. At the time of

the Wigmore Club 'scandal' they followed me for six days, wherever I went. Then they hovered, waiting and hoping for me to be sacked from the Guards Polo Club as a result. This happened in May 1988, perfectly timed during Windsor Horse Show week. Geoffrey Cross, the chairman, showed the true meaning of friendship by insisting that I carried on as normal in my duties. I didn't leave the Guards Polo Club until the following October, and when I did it had nothing to do with the Wigmore Club. Each day stories would fly around that I had gone, yet I would still be there the following Sunday when the Prince of Wales was playing. It was all deeply confusing for them.

In America it's an entirely different story. There the press have been nothing but co-operative. I have never had any problems with them when I've been there playing polo for charity. In their eyes, I'm the closest they can get to the Royal Family, which brings in more people to watch the matches and raises a lot more money.

While I was promoting the *Pimm's Book of Polo* I experienced some professional television training, a course called 'Ready for Media' run by Ann Ready in Los Angeles. The publishers had suggested it, and I wasn't terribly keen. I thought I knew it all. I would have much preferred to spend the day on the beach, but they wouldn't let me. I sat down facing the camera and was asked some simple questions. After ten minutes they stopped and played the video recording back to me. I was appalled. My answers, the way I was sitting in the chair, my coat all rumpled up, my tie . . . I couldn't believe how bad I was.

I said, 'Right, I take back everything I said. That was dreadful.'

For the next six hours they really put me through it, teaching me the right delivery, the right smiles, the right timing, and also how to be ready for all the difficult questions – usually about Sarah. I liked the chap who was doing it enormously, but towards the end of the six hours I began to hate him because by then he had got into the swing of things and was acting like every beastly reporter I'd ever met. Yet after this gruelling session I felt I could take on all comers. One of the things I learned was that it is very important to smile and disarm the reporter. This works a treat when difficult questions are coming up. Another tip was that, as the person being questioned, you are perfectly entitled not to answer. It is the interviewer who has to keep it going.

During the promotional tour, I had to do coast-to-coast television link-up interviews, where you sit alone in a studio with a camera. In your ear is a voice talking to you from Chicago. Ten minutes later it's Houston, then Los Angeles and so on. After I'd done fourteen of these I said, 'Stop! I must have a break.'

Later I must have stopped smiling because my friend who had been accompanying me whispered, 'Smile, smile.'

It was difficult. I noticed he was sitting with a big piece of paper, drawing something. To my amazement, he held up the paper behind the camera and I was looking at a large pair of breasts. I grinned and got on with my interviews. But I must have reverted to a state of gloom because soon I saw him drawing again. The next pair he held up were droopy, which really made me giggle. I hate to think what the people thought in Chicago, or wherever!

At the end of the interviews – there were over twenty – my heart was beating at about four hundred miles an hour, and I had to sit for a long time to wind down. I suppose people who do it the whole time can cope but I had never done this kind of marathon. Whenever they had asked me a difficult or boring question, I referred them back to the book, which threw them. It was certainly good practice for the negative press attention that would come my way in later years.

It has taken me a long time to learn, in dealing with the press, not to say too much. When they ring up now, out of interest I usually allow them to prattle on. When they come to a halt I'll say, 'It's a private matter, I've nothing to say – goodbye.'

A lot of them think I'm remarkably rude. I have even had to ban certain members of the local press from telephoning at all – I'll just put the telephone down on them, which is not my common practice.

Sometimes I even manage to laugh at what I read about myself. Last year, in an article in *Tatler*, one well-known Hampshire socialite was quoted as saying he would never invite me to dinner at his house again, although he wouldn't mind welcoming Sue. The amusing thing is that in twenty years, I've never set foot in his house, apart from taking the children to a party there.

The curious thing is that if I were the person the press has made me out to be, I'd be out there manipulating them for all they were worth.

CHAPTER SEVENTEEN

The Medium is the Massage

MAJOR RON IN MASSAGE PARLOUR
SCANDAL!

The tabloid newspapers swooped with glee when, on 8 May 1988, the *People* broke the news that I had been visiting the Wigmore Club. It was considered of such earth-shattering importance that they ran the story over five pages. You could tell how gravely they viewed its exclusivity by the way the *People* qualified its © copyright line: 'That includes you wallies at Wapping!' it printed, anxious to deter its arch rival the *Sun*.

What a story! Where else in the world would a group of newspaper editors send their reporters to stake out a place like the Wigmore Club? Where else in the world would it constitute the kind of scandal it provoked? Of course it wasn't a scandal at all, really, but the fact that I was Sarah's father, and should have known better, made it one. The story spread over five pages and included a lot of breathless 'confessions' from girls who worked at the club. I was quite offended by one description: 'The major had scabs on his body like eczema', it said. I've never in my life had eczema.

Clearly, this was a story the world was waiting for, which is why it remained tabloid news for a whole week. In some ways I thought it was quite amusing, but at the same time I was stunned by the hypocrisy of it all. While details of my so-called exploits occupied the front pages, in that same week seventy-four people were killed in three days in Beirut, and two million starving refugees fled southern Sudan. Five Sikhs were killed in Amritsar, and lorry drivers blocked the ports at Dover and Calais as part of a three-month dispute. At home, a five-month-old baby who had been kidnapped in Cardiff was reunited with her parents. If it was a royal drama you were looking for, then how about the fact that the Queen and Prince Philip, on a visit to Australia, were involved in a false fire alarm incident when smoke was observed to be pouring out of their plane? That only made four lines of an inside page. No, the big scoop was Major Ron and the Vice Girls.

If I had not been Sarah's father, my membership of the Wigmore Club, for whatever reason, would have passed without comment. Now, having built up the image of Sarah as the much-needed breath of fresh air for the Royal Family, the media had decided slowly and surely to dismantle it. Where better to start than with her family? I was an easy target which they milked for all it was worth.

As far as the Wigmore Club was concerned, that they stumbled on me was an accident. Later I heard on good authority that the press had been tipped off about a senior politician who was a regular visitor to the club. They didn't catch him; luckily for them they found me instead.

For some people, the Wigmore Club had unsavoury connotations. Although I used it for massage only, I was aware that it was used for other purposes and, on reflection, I realize that I should have stopped going there. Perhaps I was being naïve, yet if I had seen any harm in belonging to the club, would I have remained a member in my own name? I never tried to disguise my identity; the luggage tag of my briefcase spelled it out for all to see. As far as I was concerned, I was doing nothing wrong. For me, the Wigmore Club was a kind of cocoon, where I could shut myself away for an hour and think. Throughout my life I have needed places like this where I can relax away from all other demands. Also I could get a good massage at the club – and by that I mean a totally straight one. If you have a bruise, or a pulled muscle, a good massage will get right into it and sort it out, however painful. If the girl giving the massage happens to be attractive, so much the better. All men would admit to that – it's hardly revelatory.

Having spent time in hot countries I had also developed a liking for saunas. I have one in the garden at Dummer. The Wigmore Club's private sauna cubicles were perfect for a sportsman like me, with aches and injuries to cope with, especially as I got older. I was aware the club had a risqué reputation, but I never spoke to other members there. It was a private part of my life. Places like the Wigmore Club are part of everyday life for many men. There's nothing kinky or unusual about it. I never saw any handcuffs or chains! Whatever the press liked to make out, the Wigmore Club was not a brothel, although it probably wasn't totally straight either. If other things went on there – well, I haven't asked, seen or heard so I don't know. I do know that it was frequented by a lot of well-known people, including at least two national newspaper editors and statesmen. When the scandal broke, I was under enormous pressure to name names. I was offered a large sum of money to do so, but why should I? It was a private club.

In winter, I used to go there every couple of months, and more frequently in summer – perhaps twice a month during the polo season. The masseuses, who were of all different nationalities, were chosen for their ability, not their looks. Some were very good, could really work into the muscles. There was nothing sleazy about this; you didn't choose them from behind a one-way mirror. I came to know some of them quite well, but reports that I paid them in perfume were totally untrue. I may have given the odd gift; people who know me would confirm that that would be in my nature. A visit to the club would take about an hour and a half including the sauna. As far as I'm concerned, the 'scandal' that

Above: Out in front. The Life Guard
Mounted Squadron, Hyde Park.

Right: The Life Guard Ball.
The organizer.

Below, left: Marrying Susan at
Chelsea Register Office, the mothers
bringing up the rear.

Below, right: Susan with her parents.

Proud sister Sarah with
half-brother Andrew.

Below: Andrew's christening – Sarah and
my mother take turns with the baby.

Doting mother
with her
firstborn, aged
one year.

On the occasion of
Ayesha's christening in
the garden at Dummer.
Baby Ayesha on the
right is aunt to baby
Eliza on the left.

Escorting the Princess
of Wales to a trophy
presentation at
the Guards Polo Club.

Eugenie's christening at
Sandringham.

The team outside Dummer. Eliza is hanging on for dear life.

The red team at home.

My favourite photograph of Andrew, Alice and Eliza.

Last-minute adjustments to the dress.

The infamous train.

Andrew and Sarah returning to Buckingham Palace.

With Her Majesty
the Queen after the
wedding.

'What do we hear?'
Kiss, please.

The honeymoon coach.

At a dinner with Susan.

Skiing with the family.

The family all together
for Jane's marriage to
Rainer Luedecke.

Wentworth, August 1994.

rocked the nation was a storm in a miniature teacup. The fact that my daughter was married to the Duke of York gave the press the excuse to blow it into a hurricane.

On the evening of Saturday 7 May, James Whitaker telephoned to tip me the wink that the story was going to appear the next day. That Sunday I was playing polo with the Prince of Wales at Smith's Lawn. The press, hanging around in the hope that he would fall off, turned up in much greater numbers when they realized I was there and, seemingly, accessible. The result was press chaos, and I tried to carry on as normal. I thought I had better speak to the Prince of Wales about the presence of so many reporters. I explained what had happened.

'So what?' he said. 'Let's play polo.'

Later, Colonel Watt, chairman of the Guards Polo Club, sidled up to him behind his car. I was about three feet away, so I knew what was going on.

'What do you want me to do about Ronald – and this?' he asked the Prince.

The Prince of Wales looked at him. 'About what?' he said.

'About all this scandal,' Richard Watt replied.

'I'm here to play polo,' said the Prince. 'And so is Ronald. Let's get on with it.'

The following week, the *Sun* printed a particularly hilarious cartoon. It showed a riderless horse knocking at the door of the Wigmore Club. 'We don't see the Major much any more,' said the caption. 'But his horse is a regular customer.'

I thought this was so amusing, I wanted to buy the original drawing (which I subsequently did). I dashed off a letter to the editor but I grabbed the first piece of paper to hand which happened to be Guards Polo Club headed notepaper. This was manna from heaven for the newspaper. Gleefully, the *Sun* reproduced my entire letter on its front page, the letter heading clearly stating: 'The Guards Polo Club. President:

HRH Prince Philip.' This was a stupid mistake. I should have written on plain paper, but it did not occur to me. Within a week, the Westminster licensing authority had closed the Wigmore Club. The girls continued to make money selling their 'stories' to anyone who would buy. One of them, who was paid something like £75,000 to tell all, was later employed by a northern police force until they realized who she was and sacked her. When this happened, somebody actually rang me up and asked me to make a comment!

Not long after the Wigmore Club fiasco, I was at a dinner party where the hostess started haranguing me about visiting the club.

'How could you?' she said. She called down the dining table to her husband. 'Darling, have you ever heard of this club? Have you ever visited it?'

I didn't dare look at my host. I knew if I did, he'd be sunk. I had introduced him to the Wigmore Club, and I knew he had visited it on several occasions.

'Don't be ridiculous, darling,' my host replied. 'I wouldn't dream of it.'

What I said to him in private afterwards is unprintable.

On another occasion, one evening at a business dinner, a complete stranger leaned over and punched my arm. 'I know who you are,' he said, beaming. 'You're the bugger who closed my club down.'

Again, on the top of a mountain as late as January 1992, my ski instructor said sadly, 'Oh, yes, you're responsible for closing my club.'

I said, 'What on earth are you talking about?'

'A club,' he said. 'Begins with a W.'

'My God,' I said, 'don't tell me you went there.' He told me that various clients who had booked in with him to go skiing had recommended it.

I am sure another club like the Wigmore lives again in

London somewhere; I wouldn't want to try to find it, but I'll wager that the newspaper editors and politicians who went to the original one will make damn certain that no one finds out and gets it closed down. Apart from the notoriety sparked off by my involvement with the club, I now have nowhere to go if I want to be cocooned away. At home, I'm never totally alone as I'm on call to my family, the farm staff, the telephone. The only way I can escape these days is in my car.

What was Sarah's reaction to the Wigmore Club 'scandal'? She was heavily pregnant with Beatrice at the time, and the newspapers made much of the 'shame' that I had heaped upon her head. In reality, far from being embarrassed, ashamed and cast down by it all, she simply said to me, 'Dads, hold your head up and be even more arrogant than you normally are.'

How ludicrous it is, given the events that have rocked the Tory party in 1994, to look upon something like the Wigmore Club as a scandal. It could only have happened in this country. In France, you'd probably be given a medal. As far as I was concerned, the *People* got their priorities totally wrong in May 1988. The story that should have been splashed over every headline was that, the previous day, Graham Hick had scored 405 for Worcester against Somerset – the second highest innings of the century. Now that's what I call news.

CHAPTER EIGHTEEN

The Walls Come Tumbling Down

WHEN SARAH decided to leave Prince Andrew, it was her decision, and it needed a lot of courage to do it. She never took me into her confidence or discussed it. She would have known my reaction – I would have been strongly against it. I have always made it clear that Sarah has my support, 100 per cent, but I tell her what I think – which she doesn't always like. None of what is to follow will come as a surprise to Sarah, but no one outside the immediate family has heard before what I really think about her separation from the Duke of York.

Sarah and Andrew's marriage had been in difficulties for some time – I suspect since before Eugenie was born in March 1990 – but I have to stress that I didn't know the details. When your child's marriage is in trouble, the parents are often the last to know. Sometimes your children want to protect you. There was no question of the two sides of the family sitting around discussing the problems – even in ordinary families, this would be unusual. In our case, once the wedding celebrations were over, apart from the christenings of Beatrice and Eugenie, we did not see Prince Andrew's family socially. We did not expect to.

As an example of the dwindling public support for Sarah, there had been an outcry of disapproval about a *Hello!* magazine picture spread, showing informal photographs of her and Andrew at home with the children. The problem was not only the informality, but the question mark over whether they had been paid for the article. The Palace had not been given the opportunity to vet the idea either, which hadn't gone down well with the toadies. In fact, the whole thing was Andrew's idea; he even took some of the photographs himself. Sarah went along with his decision and was wrongly accused of publicity-seeking as a result.

There were few people Sarah could talk to about her problems. A royal marriage cannot be discussed with outsiders – you can't ring up Relate and get counselled. Even her friend and confidante, the Princess of Wales, could give only limited help as by then she certainly had her own royal crosses to bear.

It did occur to me that there were parallels between Sarah's marriage and my own first marriage. In both cases, the husbands were away a lot in the armed forces. Perhaps Sarah's mother could have given her advice on how to handle long separations, but I don't know because I never discussed it with her. But Andrew's long weeks and months away at sea had a cumulatively depressing effect on Sarah. In addition to feeling isolated and fielding press criticism almost daily, she still had problems with the Palace establishment, that inner circle of senior courtiers who surround the Royal Family. She felt they had always been out to get her, and that no one was prepared to take her side. She was trying to do the best possible job she could in Andrew's absence, and was getting very little support. There are some who would no doubt dismiss all this as rubbish and say she got as much support as she needed, and that her trouble was she wouldn't listen to advice. There is probably a grain of truth in this – she did make many mistakes. I worried most about the well publicized partying and socializing, with all kinds of people. I could see how easily Sarah might become involved with opportunists, people who saw her as an easy way to get closer to the Royal Family. She is a strong character, but she is also too trusting, and can be quite easily led. She never suspects that people are going to turn on her or let her down; she thinks that others are going to treat her the way she treats them.

The real slide to disaster began with her friendship with the Texan, Steve Wyatt, and the holiday she subsequently took with him and a party of friends to Morocco in the summer of 1990. I didn't know about the holiday, although I did know a little about the friendship. I had met Steve Wyatt's mother many years before. Lynne Wyatt is a well-known Texan socialite, who is involved in a great deal of charity fund-raising; Princess Margaret had enjoyed Lynne's hospitality on several occasions at her house Allingham, in Houston. I met her there, at a dinner she was giving to raise funds for the late Sam Wanamaker's Globe Theatre project.

Sarah first encountered Steve in 1989, when he was called back from London to help his mother with her latest royal invitation. Sarah had been invited as a guest to a British Festival at the Houston Grand Opera, which coincided with my own annual visit to play polo. I did not know Steve Wyatt well, so I don't feel qualified to comment on him, but I was aware that any friendship between him and Sarah could have disastrous consequences. When I heard whispers about her extended and highly charged new social life, I decided to speak out. Sarah telephoned me to talk about Steve Wyatt and I asked her to reduce her socializing.

'Do you really feel that strongly?' she asked.

'Yes,' I said. 'I feel very strongly. Stop. Now.'

'You surely can't expect me to stay in on my own night after night,' she retorted angrily.

As a result of that conversation, Sarah did not speak to me for six months. She had wanted to hear the truth, but didn't like what she heard.

When I reminded her of this long silence recently, she said, 'Dads, you're being ridiculous, that was just circumstance, and purely coincidental.'

'No, it wasn't,' I replied. 'You resented what I said.'

Now, I wish I had had the courage to put my foot down even harder. Once a runaway train was in motion there was little I could do to stop it. There is nothing worse than looking back, two to three years on, and thinking, 'If only I'd done that...' I suppose I hoped that the friendship would die a natural death, which is exactly what happened, but too late. Other people advised Sarah to stop seeing Steve Wyatt, and they weren't spoken to for months either. Sue, too, bitterly regrets not being tougher, but she took the line of least resistance, as I did.

In January 1992, long after Steve Wyatt was off the scene, came the discovery of a package of holiday photographs featuring him and Sarah. They were published the day before she and I were due to travel to Palm Beach to a fund-raising polo match sponsored by Cartier. Sarah was representing the Motor-Neurone Disease Association, of which she is patron. Despite the strain of the adverse publicity she carried on her duties in Florida calmly, receiving a substantial cheque on behalf of her charity.

Immediately before our return flight home, Sarah had a very difficult telephone conversation with Prince Andrew. As far as I could make out, he wouldn't give her his unqualified support and it upset her deeply. Subsequent allegations about some 'crazy' behaviour on the aeroplane were grossly exaggerated. Newspapers reported that she had been smoking, yet we were in non-smoking seats. They reported some ridiculous antics. She may have emptied a sachet of sugar into my lap, but that was all. The way that story was embroidered – by the three journalists with us in first class and the five in business class – convinced me more than anything else that the press was out to discredit my daughter.

Was there a conspiracy? It does seem strange that a package of quite important photographs could be just left behind on the top of a wardrobe in a rented flat. The real truth about this 'discovery' has never really emerged.

The following weeks were miserable; Sarah and I had few conversations about the state of her marriage, and a lot was going on behind the scenes that I didn't know about. She finally made the decision that she could not continue, and rang to warn me of the announcement I knew by then to be inevitable.

On 19 March 1992, after discussions with lawyers, the Palace announced the separation. Although the official statement was relatively innocuous, there was a furore when the same day, the BBC filed a report on *The World at One* citing an 'unidentified Palace source' as saying, 'The knives are out at the Palace for Fergie.' It went on to comment that Sarah was employing a public relations company to brief the *Daily Mail*, that the Queen was very upset with her, and that other members of the Royal Family thought she was unsuitable to be part of the family. I was furious and rang Sir Robert Fellowes, and told him how monstrous I thought it was that Charles Anson, the Queen's Press Secretary, had been allowed to make such comments. Although the remarks were not directly attributed to him, their source was obvious; even if he had thought he was speaking off the record, it was unforgivable. Eventually, after some hard intervention from Prince Andrew, as well as Sarah and myself, the statements were retracted. Charles Anson did grovel his apologies and offer his resignation, but the Queen wouldn't accept it.

I refused to speak to anyone about the separation. I couldn't believe the number of hours reporters spent waiting outside the Royal County of Berkshire Polo Club trying to get a story out of me. My office window was only fifty yards from the road, enabling photographers with long lenses to take the most boring pictures of me sitting at my desk.

On 9 April, Sarah went off on a month-long trip to Asia with Beatrice and Eugenie. I only found out about it the day before, when I called into Sunninghill Park for tea and found it awash with suitcases. She was still living there while the details of the separation were being worked out. She felt the walls were closing in around her, she said, and had to get away. She knew I wouldn't approve – which is why she hadn't told me. She was right. When she told me where she was going, and where she planned to stay, I couldn't believe it. For a start, I thought it quite unnecessary to take such little children half-way round the world. They would have been perfectly happy at home with their nanny. It seemed an unreal extravagance to go off to the Far East, and I was sure there was more to it than met the eye. I went home and told Sue, adding that I hoped John Bryan wasn't going with her. He wasn't – at least, not at the beginning.

John Bryan had masterminded the trip, however; his plan was to join her in Thailand. Bryan had first come into Sarah and Andrew's lives as their financial adviser, but as a result of his friendship with Sarah, the expression 'financial adviser' would later take on a whole new meaning in popular culture.

At the beginning, when Sarah and Andrew needed help with negotiating the rights to Sarah's *Budgie* books and the cartoon series that would stem from them, John Bryan, a friend of Steve Wyatt's, was just the man. He had several business interests, including a health-care company in Frankfurt, and was good at making financial matters seem simple. He is physically tough, as well, having been a ski instructor and a keen ice-hockey player in his day. Over a period of months, John had become highly regarded by Prince Andrew, who trusted him and listened carefully to his advice.

I was rather doubtful as to John's intentions in helping them, for the same reasons I had been suspicious of Steve Wyatt's. Obviously self-interest played a part. Then, when Sarah and Andrew parted, I felt desperately sorry for Andrew; John Bryan was seen as an intermediary between Sarah and Andrew, but I knew he had a double motive. It upset me to stand by and watch Andrew being taken in, going along with all of it, not being able to see through the situation. He believed that Sarah's emotional problems stemmed from severe postnatal depression after the birth of Eugenie. Sarah's therapist is convinced of this too. I disagree strongly. To me it is obvious that with Andrew away at sea, she was bored; first Wyatt and then John Bryan were around as a diversion. Even when Andrew was at home, he preferred to watch television rather than listen to Sarah's problems.

With the marriage in tatters and the separation details to be worked out, Sarah needed someone to help her. Unfortunately, John Bryan fell for her at the same time. When Sarah moved from Sunninghill Park to a rented house, Romenda Lodge, in Wentworth, John assisted with details like staff contracts, rental negotiations, security, confidentiality agreements. Yet I wish Sarah had turned to me for advice – at least my motives would have been straightforward. I didn't exactly resent his involvement, but it worried me and I did feel somewhat usurped.

As if the separation itself hadn't been bad enough, August 1992 saw the publication of the notorious *Daily Mirror* photographs of Sarah and John Bryan on holiday in the South of France. My first reaction was one of horror that such photographs existed of Sarah behaving in this way, especially in front of Beatrice and Eugenie; my second was of extreme anger at John for allowing it to happen. It is true that Sarah had readily agreed to go to the South of France with him, but it was John who had organized it. My third reaction was of disgust that the *Daily Mirror* had seen fit to publish the photographs in the first place. They claimed it was in the national interest; in reality, it was the *coup de grâce* in their long-running circulation war with the *Sun*.

Two days before the photographs were published, John Bryan rang me to say he was off to court to try to get an injunction against the newspaper. He failed, and I remember seeing him on the steps of the court on television that evening. At that time, he was fairly cool – he hadn't realized just how incriminating the pictures were going to be. The following morning he rang in a state of agitation; he had seen the photographs, and, as the world was soon to discover, they left little to the imagination. By this time, caught like a fly in a spider's web, Sarah was at Balmoral with Beatrice and Eugenie for the annual royal summer holiday.

Sarah likes being at Balmoral for the freedom it affords. The restrictions of a royal household are still there, but you don't feel them. She loved the wide open spaces of the countryside surrounding the castle, the less formal atmosphere. However, that morning at breakfast, the atmosphere must have been pretty icy. The timing couldn't have been worse.

Surprisingly, the person who did least to condemn her was Prince Philip. As a non-conformist himself, he would have shrugged his shoulders and said, 'There but for the grace of God go I.' When she first married Andrew, Sarah had got on well with him because she was one of the few who would stand up to him. He seemed to admire her high spirits and her feistiness, although officially he couldn't acknowledge that. He couldn't support her openly over the latest débâcle because he had to be seen to support his own son.

Seeing those pictures of my daughter was much worse than anything derogatory the papers had been able to drag out about me over the years. It is one thing to defend oneself, but when the subject is a member of your intimate family, the pain is indescribable. People had believed the financial adviser story – now they felt betrayed, made fools of by John Bryan. It was all the more shocking that Beatrice and Eugenie were in the photographs.

At the time, Sue and I discussed whether this was another example of a conspiracy to discredit Sarah, and whether the publication of the pictures had been a set-up. Yet if this were so, it would have come out by now. Since John Bryan has attacked the press so much, they would have made sure of revenge if it had been there to be taken.

Until now, my thoughts on the subject of Sarah and Andrew's separation have not been well known. My view is that they needed more time. There were faults on all sides, but there was no give and take, no room for compromise. Prince Andrew's behaviour towards Sarah throughout all of this has been impeccable, and I have the greatest respect for him. You have to take into account that royal children were brought up differently from most people – they didn't have much warmth or affection; their father wasn't the kind of man who believed in giving his children hugs and kisses. Andrew needed to be a stronger character in the face of his family and with Sarah. He should have sat her down and said, 'Come on now, this is absolutely ludicrous, you must learn to conform and stay within the boundaries of the Royal Family.' He should have stood up to her more – Sarah is a strong character. And I have to admit that when it comes to defending her in front of most members of his family, or the Palace establishment, Andrew tends to back away. Until he can summon up the courage to fight for her, Sarah knows what would happen if she ever went back. There is no question that they are extremely fond of each other, but she needs him to be 100 per cent on her side.

How much more could I have done to avert the various crises? Sarah is strong-willed, but I wish we had sat down and talked things through more. It is always easier to be objective, to work out the consequences of other people's behaviour more easily than your own. I know I've made mistakes, to put it mildly, but that doesn't mean I can't see where other people are going wrong.

Take the incident at Royal Ascot, the first year after the separation. Sarah thought it would be fun to take the children down to the change-over point to wave as the royal carriages passed by. I thought it was undignified and unnecessary.

Typically, she didn't consider the consequences – that the episode would be construed by the press and a lot of other people as Sarah saying, 'If I'm not going to be in there, I'm still determined to be a part of it.'

Andrew was trying hard to support her at the time, so he attempted to defuse the situation by being present himself the next day, but by then the damage had been done.

My final opinion is that nothing is over until it has officially been ended. I would be delighted if Sarah went back to Andrew tomorrow. I accept it would be difficult for her, however much she wanted to make the marriage a success, but if Andrew could guarantee his support, it would go a long way to solving their problems. Sarah would obviously first need to sever all connections with John Bryan, including advice on business deals.

My personal forecast is that one day she will go back. Why not? They still care deeply about each other. Their daughters are only five and three. Has separation brought happiness to either the Prince or the Princess of Wales? I doubt it. I know it has not provided lasting stability for Sarah either.

I did have the opportunity for a proper conversation with Prince Andrew in early 1994. One afternoon, I went to collect Eliza from Sunninghill Park where she had been having tea with Beatrice and Eugenie. Andrew was at home, and we sent the children into the garden so that we could talk. I had seen him a few months before, when he and Sarah had met up for tea at Dummer with the children on their way back from separate weekend engagements. I had been impressed then by how natural they were together, and how good he was with all the children. The affection that still existed between them was obvious to see. At the time it had depressed me: I thought it was a sad waste of family life.

Talking to him again at Sunninghill, I was again impressed with the way Andrew had developed. His time at the Naval Staff College, his taking command of his own ship had given him much more confidence. I told him how sorry both Sue and I were about the separation, and how much we hoped Sarah would return one day to Sunninghill Park. His reply and the major part of this conversation must remain confidential, but I was glad of the opportunity to express my thoughts.

'As far as I'm concerned,' I said, 'you haven't put a foot wrong since the separation. If it hadn't been for her involvement with John Bryan, in my opinion, she would be back with you by now.'

I've always liked Andrew, but now I admire and respect him as well. He's a different character from when he and Sarah separated. He's much tougher; if she went back he would be better equipped to handle her.

CHAPTER NINETEEN

Lesley Player

ON 9 NOVEMBER 1990, at noon, I had an appointment that was to have far-reaching consequences. I was sitting at my desk at the Royal County of Berkshire Polo Club when in walked Miss Lesley Player. She had arranged to see me to discuss her proposal for a Ladies' International Polo Tournament, something that had never been done before. Having been turned down by the Guards Polo Club and Cowdray Park, we were Miss Player's last resort. I concluded that she had a good idea. I took it up a few days later with the chairman, Bryan Morrison. I knew that one big international polo tournament could really put our club on the map. The plan got the green light and we swung into action.

The Ladies International Tournament, together with a ball at Royal Holloway College, Egham, and a dinner at the Royal Berkshire Hotel, Ascot, was to be a six-day event that would bring ladies' teams into Britain from fourteen countries. As well as providing entertainment, it could be used as an excellent vehicle to raise funds for charity – in particular, Save the Children. We knew that it would be hard work to set it up, and that it wouldn't make a great deal of money in the first year, but according to our projections, years two and three could be very successful. The club would treat it as a sponsored event, for which we would receive a fee, as is usual in such circumstances.

The Ladies' Polo Tournament took place the following August, and over the planning period both Sarah and I got to know Lesley Player quite well. She was running an employment agency in London. She also had a few personal problems, with which we tried to help. I suppose I provided a shoulder for her to cry on. On reflection, I was too trusting and very naïve. There was no great love affair between us. There may have been a silly old man's obsession, but that's a different matter. Now I wish I had never set eyes on her, let alone got involved with her. Lesley had an apparently vulnerable personality that disguised a fiercely ambitious character – unfortunately Sarah and I were both taken in by her.

Lesley worked hard to make the tournament a huge success, but it couldn't have happened without my involvement and the backing of the Royal County of Berkshire Polo Club. She may have been the brains behind it but I ran the event, together with the hard-working RCBPC staff. However, Lesley received all the accolades.

The Ladies International could have gone from strength to strength. That it never happened again had little to do with any relationship between Lesley Player and me. If I were off the scene, somebody else could have run it. The truth is that its image was severely damaged in April 1992 when the *Sunday Times* carried an article implying that there had been improper financial dealings behind the scenes. The Charity Commissioners investigated the accounts, and found everything in order. But mud sticks. Lesley Player became high profile to the media, who began digging for dirt.

Shortly after the *Sunday Times* article, the *News of the World* published a story as told by one of Lesley's ex-secretaries, detailing an alleged love affair between us. Once the sponsors got wind of the 'scandal', they rapidly withdrew their support. The Royal Berkshire certainly didn't want that kind of publicity, or indeed any further involvement. That was the end of the tournament.

I was disgusted at the way my trust had been betrayed, and even more annoyed with myself for being so easily led. For instance, immediately after the polo tournament, Lesley asked me if she might approach Sarah to help her with another venture, a children's clothing business. Stupidly I agreed that Beatrice and Eugenie might be able to model some of the clothes at a charity fashion show to be held at the Langham Hotel. I knew at the time that this was a bad idea; I should never have allowed her to suggest it to Sarah but Lesley is a persuasive person.

After the article appeared in the *News of the World* I heard rumours that Lesley was planning to write a book. By then, I was not in contact with her, but I did make a point of telephoning her when I heard this, and she vehemently denied it. Over the following nine months, I did not see or speak to her, but rumours of a possible book persisted. Then, in February 1993, when I was umpiring at a polo tournament in Helsinki, Lesley tracked me down by telephone at my hotel. She coolly informed me that the serialization of her book would begin the following Sunday in that last bastion of English truth and decency, the *News of the World*. I spent the rest of that weekend in a severely depressed state. I had no idea what would be facing me when I returned.

I discovered all too soon, and I had to laugh. In her book Lesley accused me of having terrible legs and of being poorly endowed. Pure fiction, I assure you – in fact, I've always been rather proud of my legs and as to the other, no one has ever complained before. She also said that Sarah and I had both let her down. The truth is actually the opposite. I don't want to make any more comment, because to do so would be hurtful to my family, who have already had to put up with quite enough from me. It is not so much my actions that have hurt them, as the way my actions have been interpreted by the press. Whatever went on between Lesley Player and myself was unimportant and quickly over. Without the press it would have remained private and been equally quickly for-gotten.

Most damaging of all – at least for a time – was the

ostracism I suffered. Now I'm called 'the disgraced Major Ferguson'. When I read that in the newspapers, I don't pay attention any more; I've grown used to it, but Sue, normally so calm, gets quite stressed out.

What have I been 'disgraced' over? Membership of a massage club? A stupid, short-lived obsession with a disloyal person?

CHAPTER TWENTY

Charity Tours to America

I HAVE BEEN TAKING a team to America to play polo for charity for ten years, but my first associations with polo there go back more than thirty, when I went out with a team organized by Lord Cowdray in 1962, taking our own horses. We first played at Milwaukee, where sport was limited owing to the horses getting a bad cough virus, before we moved on to Oakbrook, near Chicago.

The Oakbrook Polo Club was the home of the Butler family, who were to play a large part in my life thereafter. In 1962, Paul Butler was the Club's patron. The polo was organized by his daughter, Jorie, who later married Geoffrey Kent, who ran the Windsor Park polo team for the Prince of Wales for many years. During that first tour we stayed at the Drake Hotel. On one occasion our team, being young and high-spirited, behaved rather badly in the swimming pool. As team manager, I was summoned to a breakfast meeting with Jorie by Paul and Michael, Jorie's brother, where I was given a frightful rocket. Jorie was an absolute dragon. From that day, however, we became good friends and I have affectionately called her 'Dragon' ever since.

My association with the Butler family continued for many years and I was devastated when I heard that Paul Butler, then in his eighties, had been killed on the main road outside his house. Surely one deserves to die peacefully at such a great age? After Jorie moved away, the polo was run by Michael, and we played at Oakbrook, with different teams, many times.

Now that I no longer have any administrative duties to the game in England, I only play polo in America. Apart from the fun of staying in different American cities and meeting some charming American polo players, we raise enormous sums of money for charities such as the March of Dimes, equivalent to our Birthright. In 1992, for example, we raised $375,000 and, in 1993, over $500,000.

The team players are considerably younger than me, they're men I've known for some time, whom I know I can trust. Oliver Ellis, who is unquestionably one of my best and most trusted friends, has been a regular team member for ten years. During the last three years, the team has consisted of Andrew Seavill, William Hine, Oliver Ellis and myself. They're all good polo players, and can ride anything brilliantly. More often than not, they get more out of the horses that are lent to them than the owners themselves.

By taking relatively young up-and-coming players, it makes me look better too; I obviously can't play as hard and as fast as I used to, but the young team gets me through. We have an extremely good track record, but the winning or losing doesn't really matter because what we aim to do is to show the best side of English polo to both the American players and the audience. This not only encompasses the way we play, and our behaviour on the ground, but it also includes our behaviour off the ground when we act as ambassadors for the sport at the charity receptions and press conferences.

Travel organization is relatively simple – complimentary tickets are made available by TWA, and in the past British Airways, American Airlines and Continental have done likewise. Hotels donate rooms, on a bed-and-breakfast basis and BMW and Cadillac generously loan us cars to get us around – it's their way of supporting the charities concerned.

We start off in Atlanta, which is masterminded by Doug Matthews, co-chairman with John Wilson of the Atlanta

Polo Classic. Kathy Caputo, who used to be Doug Matthews's personal assistant, has always done a marvellous job in making sure we were at the right place at the right time, wearing the correct clothes, and with the appropriate transport laid on. Without her, the event probably couldn't take place. Also in Atlanta, we have an annual golf match, arranged by Pat Domenicon. He is the main Cadillac dealer who also happens to own the polo ground. In the autumn of 1993 he lent me his fabulous ponies, for which I was very grateful.

Whilst playing in Point Clear, Alabama, we were the guests of Kenny and Barbara McClean, and stayed at the fabulous Marriott Grand Resort Hotel, where the general manager, John Irvin, kindly put us up in the height of luxury. There are two superb golf courses in the grounds of the hotel, where we play on non-polo days. Oliver, Andrew and I are much the same handicap, but William we see only on the tee and then again on the green. In the meantime he has taken three and we have heard much crashing in the undergrowth and frightened cries from local squirrels. It's a great place to play polo and relax at the same time. Kenny has a fine string of ponies he lent me on several occasions. The main beneficiary of charity matches played there has always been American Cancer Research.

We have been going to New Orleans for the past eight years where Jennifer and Tim Rice own the fabulous Innisfree Polo Club, fairly new grounds at Folsom, over the causeway from New Orleans. New Orleans is one of our favourite stops – we love to visit the French quarter and, in particular, our friend Joe Sinatra's Old Absinthe club, the oldest bar in North America which we immediately rechristened the 'Old Arsehole'. Situated on the appropriately named Bourbon Street, it is cooled by fans instead of air-conditioning. You can sit with a delicious glass of Chardonnay and listen to wonderful classic New Orleans jazz. Joe (no relation to Frank) is a keen polo player with twenty marvellous ponies. He has been a great friend to the team in lending them to us for many years.

We've also been generously entertained in New Orleans by Bob Edmundson, a local player who has frequently wined and dined us, and smoothed our way. Another of our home-from-homes has been the Bombay Club, superbly run by Marc Turk. We have stayed at the Melrose a couple of times. Run by Mervyn Jones, it is a tranquil, well-positioned hotel with a fabulous swimming-pool. In October 1993, we stayed at Cynthia Reeves's guest house. Cynthia used to play polo and keep ponies, but she has now decided that her large house and her time would be better spent by taking in paying guests – it has been extremely successful. Biff Jones has also been a great host, both at his polo club and at his lunches at the Royal Orleans Hotel.

We have visited New Jersey twice – in 1993, we managed to win by one goal in a hard, brutal match. We play at a private ground, the Hidden Pines Polo Centre, belonging to John Rosado in Berlin, one hour from Philadelphia. In 1992, I was thrown off in the third chukka, broke two ribs and spent the rest of the match in an ambulance. We lost, so the score is even, and sadly the 1994 match had to be cancelled.

In California, playing at Palm Desert, Alex Jacoy and his assistant Susan Stovall make our lives much easier, organizing the Eldorado Polo Club quite brilliantly. I have been lent horses by Dr Madison Richardson, who celebrated his fiftieth birthday on Christmas Day 1993, and who is the leading eye surgeon in Los Angeles. His polo life is organized by Suzanne Peika, whom I have known for a very long time, having first met her at one of the Oakbrook matches.

When we played in Houston, Texas, we would arrive from our previous location on the morning of the match. This meant we had to fly in, get to the ground at noon, change, and only then were we presented with the horses on which we were to play. The matches there have always been extremely needle, so I'm eternally grateful to Charlie Flanders, polo manager at Houston, who has done a superb job over the years, and would arrange for us to ride better horses than the locals on this excellent ground.

At Newport Rhode Island, we played against a ladies' team of Susan Stovall, Stefanie Powers and Oatsey Baker. This was in aid of the William Holden World Wildlife Fund. In September 1993, we went back to Newport with a full team. Unfortunately it rained solidly for days, but we just managed to play and narrowly win. The club there is doing a terrific job on a shoestring, ably run by Dan Keating and his friend Tylor Marking.

One of the more challenging tours I have been on was sponsored by sunglass manufacturers, Revo, in aid of the Shakespeare Globe Theatre. Masterminding the tour was the late Sam Wanamaker, whose 'baby' was the new Globe Theatre project in London. We had to travel by private plane to take in all the locations where he wanted to raise money in America. Through various connections, Sam managed to persuade Carol Montgomerie, daughter of Revo's president, to lend us the Revo Lear jet. This meant that over a few days we travelled to Los Angeles, Santa Barbara, Palm Desert, Houston, and Phoenix, Arizona, in aid of the appeal. The routine at each place was the same: we would fly in, jump into a car, go to a reception, play polo, fly off again. It was incredibly tiring, but very rewarding.

In addition to playing, for seven years running I was invited to umpire the Polo World Cup in Florida. I was pleased and honoured because it meant that the American authorities were acknowledging the Hurlingham Polo Association's methods of umpiring, and obviously appreciated that we were trying to do as good a job as possible.

When a local club invites us to play, I like to think that we have done more than simply raise money for charity, although I am immensely proud of our role in that. I have tried to help the clubs in their general organization and presentation, and in particular with the way that cups and trophies are awarded. The audience for our matches is growing, and the circuit we are on is becoming more established.

When things have gone wrong in my life, it has been refreshing to be accepted simply as a person bringing over a polo team, not to be questioned or hounded by an intrusive press but to be accepted for myself, although I have to admit that being Sarah's father has added a little bit more to the occasion. It has been a joy to be welcomed in America, play the matches, get on with the job in hand. It is also a relief not to be instantly recognized, as I am in Britain.

Throughout the English polo season, whenever any of my America team mates is losing or not playing particularly well, the cry goes up, 'Roll on, Alabama.' At the end of the season, it makes a wonderful break to go off and still play the game, but in relaxed circumstances. On a recent tour, after I had been shunned by the polo fraternity in Britain, it was tremendous to feel wanted by the polo world in America, who still appeared to appreciate what I was trying to do. It is my idea of a holiday – I love the travel and the organization. There is a great sense of achievement in raising money – not only noting the appreciation of the charity organizers, but seeing the faces of the recipients themselves when we have visited children's homes, or invited young patients on to the polo ground. The hospitality and warmth of the people we meet is fantastic. I shall certainly continue to take a team on these tours as long as they want us, and as long as I can stay on a horse.

CHAPTER TWENTY-ONE

Cricket's the Thing

THE END OF THE ROAD for polo and me in Britain
came in March 1993. I had left the Royal Berkshire, and it had
been made clear to me that the Prince of Wales no longer
needed my services as his Polo Manager. After nearly forty
years of living and practically breathing polo, to say I had a gap
in my life would have been the understatement of the century.
With absolutely no sporting commitments for the summer, it
was vital for my state of mind and my morale to find something physical to do. I could have taken golf seriously, or I
could take up cricket again. Since I was always better at cricket
– the decision was easy. I had first started playing at Ludgrove
in 1940, but didn't really develop as a cricketer until I went to
Sandhurst. Like so many Etonians, I was a slow developer at
cricket: a lot of my contemporaries went on to become good
cricketers only after they had left school.

Until last year I hadn't played seriously for twenty-five
years, and no doubt some people thought it was ridiculous of
me to try to get back into playing form at sixty-one. Maybe
they were right, for I found it a damn sight harder than I could
possibly have imagined. I thought I could just waltz in and
play. Far from it. Years of injuries on the polo field had taken
their toll, my knees were painful and creaky, I couldn't run
much, and my bowling arm felt leaden. Undeterred, I dug out
my old cricket equipment and found a mouse nesting in the
pads! I rushed off to our excellent local sports shop in Alton to
get kitted up nineties style, and bought myself a new Koo-
kaburra bat for good measure.

I needed some coaching to get me back in the swing of things. I am a life member of Hampshire Cricket Club, so I rang up the Southampton County Ground and asked the secretary for a recommendation. He suggested I rang Peter Sainsbury, the ex-chief coach for Hampshire.

When Peter got my message on his answerphone, he thought someone was playing a joke on him, and he still didn't really believe it was me until we met. After a couple of practice sessions, things started to go better for me, with batting at least.

'I didn't know what to expect,' Peter said. 'You came into the nets and you didn't have any defence. All you were interested in was hitting the ball.'

After a few more weeks of steady practice in the nets, Peter admitted my defence had improved so much that he had a hard time getting me out. I'm grateful to Mark Nicholas, captain of the Hampshire team and a friend of Sarah's, for his co-operation in allowing me to use the nets in the first place.

I used to be a good bowler, but when I broke my neck I also pulled out two tendons in my arm. That was a long time ago, but the bowling action puts a lot of pressure on the shoulder and upper arm. My arm will never be strong, but I am learning to adapt my action, encouraged by my knees being a good deal less painful. For this, I am indebted to Josh Salzmann, an American fitness instructor who works at the tennis section at Wentworth Golf Club. In his early thirties, unfailingly cheerful, he has been a great help to Sarah in helping her to keep fit. The weight loss she achieved after the birth of Beatrice was thanks to Josh, and Sarah has continued his exercise routines ever since.

On Sarah's recommendation, I asked Josh if he could help me to sort out the aches and pains in my knees. Now I work out with him at the gym once a week, using weights machines and doing floor exercises, starting with a mile and a half on the treadmill. I like Josh enormously. He has also given me a programme of exercise to do at home, to keep up the good work. My knees are so much better that when I played polo in America last year I was able to do without knee bandages for the first time in ten years. I could play a six-chukka match without any discomfort, either during or after.

Having established that I could actually play cricket, I then rang up the chairman of our local Farleigh Wallop Club and said, 'If you'd have me, I'd very much like to come and play with you.' I think they were most surprised.

Unfortunately, the news got out, and on the day of my first match for Farleigh Wallop, photographers and reporters turned up at the cricket ground. They came wandering in, cameras at the ready. I asked them what they were there for.

'We gather you're playing,' they said.

'Yes, I am, but this is a private ground and you're not welcome. Would you please leave.'

'That's very unsporting of you. We're only here to take photographs.'

I knew perfectly well that if they went down to the public road bordering the cricket ground they could take as many pictures as they liked, which, of course, they did. But more than anything else, I was anxious to reassure the team that having me on board would not mean turning every match into a media circus. As it was the first time I had played with them, they could easily have thought it wasn't worth the hassle.

I also play for Oakley, but in the first match I was out first ball, and out for one in the second. They can't possibly want me, I thought, but they did. I made a few runs after that and felt much better. Playing cricket with such genuine, friendly people has been an eye-opener for me. To all the village players I am known as Ron, except for one player at Farleigh whose family have lived in Dummer all their lives. He still calls me Major Ron.

How my fellow cricketers must have wondered about this

geriatric non-bowler who could barely run around the out-field! Last year I also played with the Eton Ramblers (some of whom weren't even born when I was at Eton), the Guards Cricket Club, the Butterflies team, made up of old boys from Eton and four other public schools. I found I was often the only player over the age of thirty.

The reason I won't go to a polo ground any more is not because of the game, but the people involved in it. Most of them are extremely superficial. When I was of use to them, many were fawning all over me. Now they don't want to know. So much for friendship. Since I left the Royal Berkshire and ceased my duties to the Prince of Wales, I haven't had a single telephone call from any of my 'friends' in the polo world, including all those whom I helped to get started in the game.

The village cricket teams have gone a long way to restoring my faith in humanity. The people are kind and accept me for what I am. I have felt very comfortable playing with them – they make jokes about me and aren't in awe of me. It is clear that my future won't be with the polo set, or the Hampshire set, or the Royal Family, but with the many delightful local people I count myself fortunate to have discovered.

Now I'm excited about the prospect of organizing an indoor cricket school at Dummer. Having lived in this area for so long, it is a way of giving something back to the community. There is a real need for indoor cricket facilities in this part of North Hampshire. I hope it will help all the younger boys and girls who want to play, and who cannot because of the swingeing cutbacks in the sport within the local schools.

I have a large barn on the farm where the cows used to winter. When Oakley Cricket Club said they wanted to organize a barn dance, I offered to lend it to them. Then as the committee meeting went on, and conversation turned to Colts and lack of facilities, it suddenly dawned on me that the barn would be ideal for a cricket school. One thing led to another, and now we plan to open the Dummer Indoor Cricket School in November 1994.

CHAPTER TWENTY-TWO

One Happy Ending

THE BREAK-UP of Jane's marriage was fraught with difficulties and complications, and for a while she was at a low ebb. I was frustrated at being able to do so little for her as she was thousands of miles away in Sydney. I was therefore delighted when I heard about the new man in her life, Rainer Luedecke. The children call him Rhino – the way his name is pronounced.

I first met Rainer at Christmas 1991 when he literally jumped out from behind my drawing-room curtains! Jane was coming for Christmas with him and her children, Seamus and Ayesha, and they arrived secretly at Dummer a day earlier than I had expected them. The whole thing was kept as a big surprise for me, though everyone else knew, including my children and the farm staff. When they heard me approaching, they all rushed to hide – somewhat embarrassing for poor Rainer who had yet to be formally introduced!

Jane had met him at a dance in Sydney. It was a set-up: at the time Jane was not remotely interested in renewing her social life. One of her girlfriends thought otherwise and dragged her off to the dance, assuring her she would be escorted by someone she knew well. What happened was that Rainer, a marketing and advertising consultant, was brought along as a blind date for Jane. She jokes that she spent the first hour in his company struggling to help him tie his bow-tie. Their relationship developed slowly and steadily: Jane had no wish to rush into anything this time round, and Rainer was patient. Over the years I had got to know him quite well by speaking over the telephone, and I liked him from the start. I was grateful to him for having looked after Jane so well, and for giving her the moral support she needed through all the adversities she had had with Alex and the children, not to mention the press in Australia.

Rainer proposed to Jane in early 1993. He rang me in my office at the Royal Berkshire to tell me that she had accepted, and to ask what I thought of it. I was delighted. Rainer is a man in a million: he's intelligent, an all-round sportsman and tremendous with Seamus and Ayesha, setting himself up as a friend rather than a father figure. He is of German origin – his parents emigrated in 1946. He's very direct and speaks his mind, Australian-style.

Jane made a visit to England in April 1993, and at that time, she and Rainer had not decided when or where they were going to get married. He wanted to finish a law degree, which would qualify him to practise as a lawyer, and Jane needed to clear up the custody situation regarding her children.

'Whenever and wherever the wedding is,' Jane said firmly, 'we must bring the whole family together.'

Sometime during that summer, Jane and Rainer decided they would marry on New Year's Day 1994, and that Seamus would give her away. Her daughter Ayesha, along with Alice and Eliza and Sarah's two, would all be flower girls. It was a wonderful dream, and I could hardly believe it was going to happen when the plans were being made last autumn. Sue spent hours planning the girls' dresses with her business partner, Sybil Fleggson. Sue and Sybil run a children's and baby clothes business called Beloved, and it was their inspiration and talent that went into the lovely smocked dresses in Liberty print that the girls would wear on the day. Jane did wonders with Qantas: even though it is their busiest time of year, she managed to arrange tickets so we could fly out on 18 December and spend a couple of weeks together before travelling back on 2 January. Sarah was to follow on 29 December with Beatrice and Eugenie.

We were so disappointed that my mother's bad hip meant that the long flight to Australia was out of the question for her. Though she would be spending Christmas with some close and dear friends, we were sad at leaving her behind on one of our happiest family occasions.

The departure date meant we flew to Australia only two days after the children got back from school, so it was quite a rush to get everything ready in time. In our drawing room, school trunks fought for space with Christmas presents and piles of summer clothes, which had had to be dug out and dusted for Australia. We had hoped to forget about Christmas decorations this year, but on Eliza's insistence a tree had to be brought in and decorated, otherwise in her words Christmas wasn't happening.

We had no idea where we were going to stay until the last minute. Jane wanted us all to be together. She rented a house for her family and ours in Palm Beach, about forty-five minutes north of Sydney, and arranged for another in the same area for Sarah. She and Rainer met us at Sydney airport accompanied by the children and their Jack Russell, Pippa, and we all piled into two Toyota minibuses for the drive to Palm Beach. The house Jane had found was overlooking the beach, but a twenty-five-minute walk or five-minute drive away as it was set on a steep hill above the sea. There was a large sitting room with a kitchen off it and a balcony with fabulous views.

For a glorious ten days we had a real family holiday. The children learned to boogie-board – a scaled-down version of surfing – and they loved swimming in the big waves. The weather was about 85°, with a good breeze, so it was never suffocating.

On Christmas Day we had a traditional lunch, for which I had shopped the day before. Preparations were made on Christmas Eve, and because all the rest of the family wanted to spend the morning on the beach, I was left in charge of the cooking – following strict instructions. It was marvellous to be surrounded by almost my entire family, dressed in casual beach clothes, eating a traditional Christmas lunch while the temperature soared in the high eighties.

Boxing Day is Alice's birthday, and Jane and Rainer had organized a boat for the day, a catamaran with an engine. We motored out to a deserted beach where we anchored for several hours. On the way back we put up the sails but just as quickly took them down again when a strong southerly wind blew up. Alice loved every minute of the day, a completely different birthday from anything she had ever experienced before.

Jane and I played golf a few times with Andrew and Rainer. I was most impressed with Jane's golf; she has a wonderful style and had made great progress in no time. Andrew played well, I less so. We played once at the Royal Sydney Golf Course. Jane had warned me that the course had 365 bunkers – I swear I got myself into 366 of them!

One of the highlights of our visit was the trip Jane arranged for us to stay with James and Sally Archibald and their three sons at their farm near Scone, New South Wales, about three and a half hours' drive from Sydney. I'd met James when he first came to England to play polo, and he and Sally had stayed with us at Dummer. On the first afternoon, James arranged enough polo ponies for us all to go out for a ride. It must have been an extraordinary sight, including, as it did, Rainer, who hadn't ridden much, Sue, who hardly rides at all, and Eliza who was a beginner. She was only used to Alice's small pony at home – now she was being led by me on a polo pony which must have seemed enormous. However, on the return journey, Eliza decided that if Ayesha didn't need a leading rein, then neither did she. The rest of the way back she rode by my side without being led.

James had borrowed a small marquee to accommodate all

the children in sleeping bags, but what we had failed to take into account was the unpredictable nature of the Australian weather at that time of year. At around midnight the heavens opened, and Sally Archibald and I went out in our nightclothes to see which of our children had been swept away! One by one they came straggling in. Alice and Eliza ended up on our bedroom floor, Ayesha crept into Jane's room, and all that were left of the brave pioneers outside were the three eldest boys who slept right through the storm and survived a spider found on a pillow.

We returned to Sydney the day before Sarah and her entourage arrived. She was accompanied by two personal protection officers, which is mandatory whenever she is with Beatrice and Eugenie. The local New South Wales police force had been alerted, so they too were around in the background. When we went to the beach with them we soon discovered the difference – not only were the policemen dancing attendance, but the press had discovered us in their usual tiresome way. We did manage to have a wonderful fish and chip lunch on Whale Beach without too much interruption, although reporters had staked out the house where Sarah and the children were staying. They followed wherever she went, and on the day before the wedding, we hired a boat to get away. The plan was that Sarah would meet us further out to sea, having been brought out by a police boat. The press still followed, in a fleet of smaller boats and even two news helicopters.

Two days before the wedding Jane gave a small barbecue party at the house. Sarah and her children came and met Rainer's parents and relatives. It was quiet, relaxed and most enjoyable.

There had been a great deal of secrecy and subterfuge surrounding the date and location of the wedding. Jane had deliberately announced in England that the wedding was to take place at Easter to throw the press off the scent, but unfortunately news that it would be New Year's Day leaked out in Australia, though no one knew the location until the last minute. Rumours circulated and various news channels reported that it was to be on an island off the Great Barrier Reef, but no one knew for sure. To try to preserve the security, Jane was not allowed anywhere near the actual location, Jonah's Hotel. Her eighty-odd guests were bussed in; as for the wording on the invitation, all they knew was that they had been invited to lunch to meet me.

We had decided not to have a New Year's Eve party. With a wedding to be got through the next day, there was no question of allowing the children to be up late. Besides, there was masses to do, for the day after the wedding we would all be going our separate ways. Sue was packing, I was doing my own ironing – much to the children's amusement – and when midnight struck, we just raised a glass to each other and went on with our chores.

The wedding went off superbly, helped by some behind-the-scenes last-minute preparations organized by Sue and by the wonderful wedding celebrant, Susan Bradley. Jane appointed me Master of Ceremonies, and the wedding was held on the terrace, with a breathtaking vista of the Pacific Ocean for a backdrop, and beautiful flowers everywhere. A week later we could not have held the ceremony there; the forest fires then raging around Sydney created so much black smoke it would have been impossible.

We were delighted that both Rainer's parents and several other relatives were present. Rainer's best man was one of his closest friends, a splendid fellow called Brett Faulkner. Brett had been a fantastic sportsman but had suffered a tragic sailboard accident and had broken his neck, leaving him a quadriplegic.

From a security point of view, Jonah's Hotel was ideal. There was a sheer cliff drop from the balcony to the sea, and the two entrances to the hotel were easy to secure. The only potentially weak link was a private house to the right.

Initially its owner had given permission for photographers to take pictures through her garden hedge. However she withdrew this rapidly after the New South Wales police told her exactly what she was letting herself in for in terms of numbers and chaos. Two photographers did position themselves high on some cliffs about a mile away, and we thought that we might be invaded by a hovering helicopter as had happened previously. The helicopter did arrive, but buzzing into view just as we were going in to lunch and out of sight.

All the children behaved impeccably. Alice, Seamus and Andrew formed one allegiance, Eliza and Ayesha the other, and the younger two did a terrific job of looking after Beatrice and Eugenie. It was very hot, and, after their special children's menu at lunch, the younger children had the added bonus of being taken off to the beach.

Seamus, now twelve, did a wonderful job of 'giving away' his mother. Ayesha, who is Eliza's age, looks very like Eliza. She's a tough little girl who rides well. Eliza isn't particularly aware that, technically, she's Ayesha's aunt; she just knows that these two are my grandchildren. Jane named Ayesha after the Maharani of Jaipur, who had lived near us at Ascot, and who had always been a tremendous supporter of Jane.

Whenever I am asked how my grandchildren are, everyone seems to think I only have two, Beatrice and Eugenie. I have to remind them about Seamus and Ayesha. We see them so rarely, so this trip was a particular thrill for all of us, and the memories of my four grandchildren together in Australia I'll treasure for ever.

Though totally different characters, Beatrice and Eugenie are both happy little girls. I suspect Eugenie will turn out to be the stronger of the two. They call me Grubby – it started when Beatrice couldn't quite get 'grandpa' out, and it's stuck. They have a sheltered upbringing but they are not spoiled, and at the moment they don't seem to have been affected by their parents' separation. I always get a very warm welcome from them both and I'm lucky that I can see them more or less whenever I like.

I said in my speech at Jane's wedding how deeply I felt that Jane deserved the happiness she has now found with Rainer. I couldn't help reflecting to myself how different it all was from her first wedding. Then I'd had to put on a brave face as she married someone I did not approve of. This time she was marrying a man who was worthy of her. Although she still has to tackle some difficulties concerning her children, I do feel that one side of her life is resolved.

I shall always worry about Jane simply because she is thousands of miles away. Now, thanks to Rainer Luedecke, I shall worry considerably less.

Epilogue

DUMMER, JULY 1994

As I sit here at my desk gazing out on to my garden throughout this glorious long hot summer, it seems there can be no
logical conclusion to this book – and certainly not the fairy-
tale happy ending I had hoped for when I first started writing
it.

I am aware that much of what I've written may seem
disappointingly anodyne to those of my readers who had
hoped for more salacious detail. There's good reason for this.
Of course I could have said more. I could have gone into
much greater depth, but I have held back for fear of jeopar-
dizing the one thing I hope for the most – that Sarah and
Andrew might be reconciled.

All year, the signs have been encouraging – as I write this
last chapter, I do honestly believe it will happen. The question is – when? I have no idea.

Why hasn't Sarah gone back to Andrew already? I suspect
it's a hesitation on her part to be drawn back into the
claustrophobic establishment atmosphere she was so relieved
to escape from. She knows that if she does go back, her
commitment has to be 100 per cent, and she must decide if
she can settle for that lifestyle again. There's no point in
going back and living separately.

I am sure Sarah is frightened of losing the independence
she's enjoyed recently, and that once again Andrew will be

unable to stand up for her and defend her. She says she's unsure of how the Palace courtiers would react – she feels the 'vibes' are still bad. She'll say, 'They're still at me.'

'How?' I ask.

'Oh, it's obvious.' She won't be specific.

My awful fear is if it did happen, how long would she be able to stay on the straight and narrow? She could not step out of line again. She wouldn't even be let off the hook by going back – she'd have to work at it. At the slightest hint of a transgression, the reptiles of the press would gleefully reiterate all her former gaffes.

I worry most, as always, about the children. At five years old, Beatrice is soon going to wonder why Mummy and Daddy aren't together all the time, because when they are, the whole family has so much fun. So far, Sarah's managed to avoid discussing details with her daughters but this won't last. Soon Beatrice will ask questions or she'll pick up gossip from children at school.

This year, for the first time since the separation, we were invited to lunch at Sunninghill Park on Easter Sunday. Andrew and Sarah and the children were there, and so were my mother and our own three children. It was the kind of happy family occasion I had despaired of ever seeing again. Although Andrew and Sarah had come for tea once at Dummer last year, they had arrived separately, and my mother hadn't been present. This year, I hoped, marked the beginning of a new era. Incidents like this give me hope, however minor – such as happy photographs of them at Windsor horse show or reports of them happy together at someone's barbecue. I've seen how much they enjoy each other's company so I know there's a basis for my hopes, although at times I could be accused of clutching at straws.

We had a really jolly time at Sunninghill. Then came the bombshell. After lunch, I told Sarah we'd better be on our way – presumably they were going to tea at Windsor Castle?

She looked at me, pulled a face and said, 'No, I'm not going. Andrew's going. Apparently the Queen wants me but the rest of the family don't.' Sarah still has a good relationship with the Queen but she doesn't appear to be on good terms with other members of the family.

I was appalled. Why couldn't the Queen, who must be the head of that household, tell the rest of them to go for a walk? Andrew was upset that Sarah had been left out but why didn't he say: 'If Sarah's not coming, then neither am I'? Probably because Sarah wouldn't want him to, for fear of creating an even bigger rift. So Andrew and the girls went to Windsor, and we went home, leaving Sarah to return alone to Romenda Lodge.

Yet if the outside world could see Andrew and Sarah together, they would fail to understand how they can be apart. You couldn't wish for a more loving couple – the way they look at each other, touch each other, laugh with the children. You drive away and think this is absolutely crazy. You ask yourself, Why aren't they together?

One of the problems is that she's grown apart from that life. The other night she said to me on the telephone: 'I'm thirty-four, nearly thirty-five and I haven't lived my life at all.'

I was sorely tempted to say, 'It's entirely your fault.' I didn't want to attack her, so I stayed silent. Sarah has had everything – more than anyone else in the world – but she threw it away. It's no good her saying she hasn't had a life, she's had a wonderful life. She's done whatever she wanted to do. What she means is she hasn't done what she wanted to do with complete freedom. But you can't have everything. No one knows that more than I do. I think Sarah does love Andrew, and he'd have her back tomorrow. His behaviour has been exemplary; he hasn't had any of the flings you'd expect a man in his position to have. The press tried to pin something on him, but they were wrong. I'll never forget the moment after Christmas when I went to collect Eliza, who'd been to tea at Sunninghill. Andrew and I were chatting, and he said: 'The doors will always be open for Sarah.' I was so touched. The truth is, he's never fallen out of love with her. He's been very long-suffering and patient. I think, given a second chance, that he'd be a much better husband. His new shore job means he would be around more – a vital pre-requisite if they do have a reconciliation.

What would they gain if they divorced? Sarah could never discard her 'disgraced duchess' image. (Any more than I can do likewise with my 'disgraced Major' tag.) If she thinks she can ever be a free spirit, she's wrong. She's the mother of the Queen's grandchildren, two princesses of the realm. She can't escape and live in another country unless she agrees to lose her children, and that could never be.

If either Andrew or Sarah remarried, it would be very difficult to be happy with anyone else – their former life together will always be there to haunt them.

Besides, what more could Sarah want from a husband? Prince Andrew is naturally good with children. He is different from all the other royals. Under Sarah's influence, he's experienced a much more natural life. He's a calmer, more affectionate person than the others, more down to earth. He has normal interests, such as photography and golf, and his friends are normal people; even those friends who are involved in show business are a lot more human than the establishment toadies. Andrew has none of the aloofness and distance of his elder brother and father. You can talk to him naturally – you just have to remember to throw in the odd 'sir' from time to time. Andrew might have been a bit pompous once, but the navy seems to have bashed that out of him. At the end of the day, despite her fears of being swallowed up by the establishment, Sarah would be much freer if she did go back. The economics would make better sense too. At the moment, there's the vast expense of maintaining two households – Andrew is racketing around in Sunninghill, while Sarah has been paying a huge rent for Romenda Lodge. Speaking of economics, Sarah would also have to get her financial affairs in order – reports of the vast amounts of money she is supposed to have made from the *Budgie* cartoon character have been grossly overestimated. I suspect that not all of the money has materialized anyway, although I haven't any facts to substantiate that.

Another setback has been the recent court case brought by Jane against John Bryan. She accused him of failing to hand over all of the fee paid by *Hello!* magazine for pictures of her wedding to Rainer, a deal which John Bryan had set up in the first place. When I wrote in the previous chapter of my joy at seeing all the family happy and together on that occasion, I must have stirred up the Ferguson fates. As an indirect result of the wedding, more family troubles have surfaced, and as usual I've been stuck right in the middle. I tried hard to resolve it without the legal expense of going to court, but to no avail. Now the case is over, there will be no appeal and the money will be paid to Jane, but all of this has created difficulties within the family. By the time this book is published, I hope Jane's relationship with Sarah will be back to normal.

Having mentioned *Hello!*, I feel I must express my admiration of the Marquesa de Varela for the unfailingly high standard of the articles which she coordinates for the magazine. We first met when *Hola!* sponsored a polo match at the Guards Polo Club to launch *Hello!* in England. She has such an attractive and lively personality, always managing to be very fair and sensitive. She succeeds in presenting happy and interesting stories, together with beautiful photographs, which everyone (however secretly) loves to read and admire.

What of the future? I can only be optimistic. My greatest wish would be to see all the younger generation of my family attain great happiness. My next greatest happiness would be to score a century before I'm too old to hold a cricket bat. Last week, I made 92 runs playing for Oakley – so who knows?

As I said, my optimism knows no bounds.

Forgetting those things which are behind, and reaching forth unto those things which are before, this is wisdom.

Philippians 3:13